Finding a Different Kind of Normal

of related interest

Pretending to be Normal
Living with Asperger's Syndrome
Liane Holliday Willey
Foreword by Tony Attwood
ISBN 1 85302 749 9

Freaks, Geeks and Asperger Syndrome
A User Guide to Adolescence
Luke Jackson
Foreword by Tony Attwood
ISBN 1 84310 098 3
Winner of the NASEN & TES Special Educational Needs Children's Book Award 2003

Build Your Own Life
A Self-Help Guide For Individuals With Asperger Syndrome
Wendy Lawson
Foreword by Dr Dinah Murray
ISBN 1 84310 114 9

Everyday Heaven
Journeys Beyond the Stereotypes of Autism
Donna Williams
ISBN 1 84310 211 0

Asperger's Syndrome
A Guide for Parents and Professionals
Tony Attwood
Foreword by Lorna Wing
ISBN 1 85302 577 1

Finding a Different Kind of Normal

Misadventures with Asperger Syndrome

Jeanette Purkis

Foreword by Donna Williams

Jessica Kingsley Publishers
London and Philadelphia

Cover artwork by Jeannette Purkis

First published in 2006
by Jessica Kingsley Publishers
116 Pentonville Road
London N1 9JB, UK
and
400 Market Street, Suite 400
Philadelphia, PA 19106, USA

www.jkp.com

Copyright © Jeanette Purkis 2006
Foreword copyright © Donna Williams 2006
Reprinted twice in 2006

Library of Congress Cataloging in Publication Data

Purkis, Jeanette, 1974-

Finding a different kind of normal : misadventures with Asperger syndrome / Jeanette Purkis ; foreword by Donna Williams.

p. cm.

ISBN-13: 978-1-84310-416-2 (pbk. : alk. paper)

ISBN-10: 1-84310-416-4 (pbk. : alk. paper) 1. Purkis, Jeannette, 1974- 2. Asperger's syndrome—Patients—Biography. I. Title.

RC553.A88P87 2006

362.196'8588320092—dc22

2005026416

British Library Cataloguing in Publication Data

A CIP catalogue record for this book is available from the British Library

ISBN-13: 978 1 84310 416 2
ISBN-10: 1 84310 416 4

Printed and bound in Great Britain by
Athenaeum Press, Gateshead, Tyne and Wear

To Donna. Thanks for making it possible.

Contents

Foreword by Donna Williams 9

1. Being in the World but Not of It 11

2. Searching for the Rules 25

3. Learning Which Way is Left 43

4. Acting, Independently 65

5. Becoming the Enemy 83

6. Losing Friends and Gaining Contacts 103

7. Watching the End of the World 121

8. Dying and Surviving 139

9. Educating the Mad 159

10. Forgetting the Script 175

Epilogue 191

Foreword

It takes a lot of guts to own up. Jeanette Purkis must then be one very gutsy person. In *Finding a Different Kind of Normal* Jeanette takes us through her various incarnations from a church-going Christian to her acceptance of being gay, to being a raving left-wing extremist and into prison and mental institutions and her eventual diagnosis with Asperger Syndrome. On the way, we also see Jeanette the artist, the loner and the optimist. Jeanette shows us much about the childhood, adolescence and early adulthood of someone with Asperger Syndrome. But Jeanette also takes us to that uncomfortable reality where Asperger Syndrome, personality disorder and outright sociopathy ebb and flow. Whilst the debate rages as to whether those with Asperger Syndrome have empathy, can lie, or are even, as we most fear, 'psychopaths', Jeanette takes us right into the heart of those questions and shows us the human face of such things and that ultimately there is a matter of 'choice' and that insight is possible, self-control, foreseeable. Hers is far from a pretty story. But pretty stories don't take us to the difficult answers. Whilst there are certainly many people with Asperger Syndrome who have had different, more 'tasteful' challenges than her, there are many families who live isolated even from the community of autism support who have children with the challenges

Jeanette has lived with and come to manage. I would recommend this book to those families and all manner of health, welfare and education professionals associated with them, and beyond this to those who simply want to learn about those dark spaces in order to better appreciate the light spaces too.

Donna Williams

Being in the World but Not of It

In south-eastern England, 1974, my birth was just what my mother had hoped for – a younger sister for my brother Dean to play with. I'm told I was an odd baby; I would not let my father touch me, I'd go rigid if he came near and only seemed to want affection from my mum. I'd stare up at the curtain rod and not look at people. My parents thought I had a problem with my eyes so they took me to the doctor who treated me for a 'squint' or lazy eye. Yet after my vision was corrected I'd still stare at the curtain rod and not at any of the human inhabitants of the room.

In my earliest dream I was in a bed in an octagonal room. There was that feel when the light is just right and the sun is shining in. The walls were white and there were no objects in the room other than me, the huge bed I was lying in and a heater mounted on the wall above my bed. It was like nothing could go wrong in the world. Then, without warning, the heater above my head dropped from the wall, hitting me and I assume killing me. During my childhood I was terrified of the unexpected, of fire, of losing control.

I admired my brother more than anyone else in the world. It was as if he owned the moon. Everything my brother did I wanted to do. He went to kindergarten, I wanted to go to kindergarten. He went to school, I wanted to go to school. I thought he was wonderful and that everything he did must be wonderful, too. When I went to kindergarten I found it did not live up to my expectations and was a scary place full of kids who moved in a world I didn't understand. They'd all play games together and I didn't know how to join in. I liked their chants – 'I'm the king of the castle, you're the dirty rascal' – but their games were somewhat alien to me. I had no idea how to join in with other children and would attack anyone who came too close. I beat up a four-year-old boy when I was three and the teacher made me sit in the corner and told the dog, a Jack Russell who I'm sure was little capable of biting anyone, to bite me. I was terrified and thought the dog would do exactly as she said. I spent the rest of the day huddled in the corner trying to avoid the dog who came over periodically to have a sniff at the little girl crouching on the floor.

When I turned four I was technically old enough to go to school. I already knew how to read and write, having been taught by some elderly friends of my parents. This couple were delightful people who strove to introduce me to the academic world they inhabited. They took me to museums and galleries, stately homes and the nearby Cambridge colleges. They took me to some mansion and explained that the spectacularly painted ceiling was 'rococo'. I thought this was such a lovely word that I said it throughout the day and probably for weeks afterwards. They also took me to the Scott of the Antarctic museum, which left me revolted for days as some mouldy chocolate from the expedition was on display. I had had a phobia about mould and decay ever since I could remember.

My school teacher was a Scottish lady who I didn't like very much and the other children were strange and rude. Try as I could I did not know 'the rules'. My brother tells me that during my first week at school I took off my dress and pulled down my underpants in the school yard and the teacher's aide came and 'dragged me away'. For some reason I had a phobia of children who had been off sick and would attack them without a second thought. I also lashed out at anyone who came too close, as I felt my world was being invaded. If another child came too near me while collecting art materials, I would punch or push them until they had left my personal space and was always surprised when I earned the wrath of the teacher for doing this; to me it made perfect sense. My reading age was years beyond my actual one and my knowledge of the subjects I was interested in, such as space exploration or fungi, was quite impressive for a five-year-old, yet it was decided I was disturbed and needed to see a psychiatrist. He was an older man with curly white hair who was always kind. I loved the painting on his office wall, which was colourful and had pictures of trees that looked like lollipops. I now had to go to a special class for special children, too. It was on Thursdays and my mum would take me from school, causing questions from the other kids. From my parents' attitude I knew there was something embarrassing about the fact that I had to go to these classes. I remember eating sand from the sink and a boy shoving my head in the sand and throwing my glasses out of the open window. That was the last time I went to Thursday afternoon class.

I loved eating mud, playing in fresh-mown grass or spinning around in circles. The best way to do this was on a sunny day looking into the sun with your eyes closed. Then you got a double whammy – your eyes were full of orange and your head was spinny and dizzy. Playing on the monkey bars was pretty good, too, providing no one else was using them. I didn't like the older kids, who treated me as if I were crazy or a bit slow. There was a boy called Jason who came from a large farming family. Jason would come up to me and say 'Suck my cock Jeanette Purkis.' The first time he said this I had no idea what he wanted me to suck but I worked it out pretty quickly. I was five. He was ten years old.

When I was five Heather was my first friend. Her biological parents had been Jamaican but she was adopted as a baby by a white English family. The other kids picked on her as she was the only black kid in the school. I had no idea of what racism was; it had never occurred to me to judge anyone on the basis of skin colour. Heather and I would sit together and draw. Her hair was unlike any hair I'd seen before and felt marvellous when I touched it. I wished I had hair like Heather's; I'd say 'I want your hair', to which she would reply 'I want yours.' When I was about seven Heather left to go to a private school. I missed having someone to talk to and compare hair with.

My brother had a girlfriend. Her name was Tara. She was a tiny girl and I could see why Dean liked her so much. I'd grab Tara and kiss her as many times as I could – on the arms, legs, face, everywhere. Dean stayed in contact with Tara all through school so I used to still see her too. I'd pick her up and kiss her even when I was 10 or 11.

I had a nemesis at primary school. Our hatred of each other was mutual and we never lost an opportunity to pick on one another or fight physically. Emily was one of Jason's many siblings. Emily was a 'tomboy' and only wore trousers. She had to wear a skirt for a school singing concert once and she burst into tears and went home rather than put it on. My mum tells me that one day I attacked Emily and strangled her. My mum came to pick me up, as I'd been suspended. She saw red marks around Emily's neck.

I was very good at befriending cats and would go to people's houses just to play with their cat. I could spend hours talking to the feline inhabitant of a house but I'd only say hello and goodbye to the human members of the family. One time my parents took me to a cattery and I was in heaven! There were hundreds of cats, all of them for sale. I went and patted as many as I could and was even sad when the lady showed me some sick cats in the vet clinic there. I had never been sad about sickness or death in people but felt for the poor, sickly cats, wishing they would get better and worrying that they might die. We'd go to people's houses after church for Sunday lunch and I'd be delighted if they had a cat. I could occupy myself for hours playing with kitty and not having to bother with talking to people. I went to visit the secretary from primary school because she'd told me she had four cats. I went there on a Sunday afternoon and spent about four hours with the cats in the garden. I went to a classmate's house, mainly because she told me she had several cats. She was a little upset that I spent most of my time there talking to the cats and the rest of it talking to her mum. I wasn't the slightest bit interested in the kinds of things children my own age had to say, yet could carry on conversations with adults about my various interests.

My interests at age eight were mainly cats and *Doctor Who*. I'd write stories about time travel and space or illustrate lengthy books with meticulous drawings of every breed of cat I knew. I would pretend to be The Doctor from *Doctor Who* and made a cardboard model Tardis to send off to a TV show called *Jim'll Fix It* in which the presenter, Jimmy Savile, would 'fix it' so kids could fulfil their desires. My letters (and there were a good many of them) always requested that I visit the set of *Doctor Who* and meet the actors. I found out, after about my tenth letter – the one in which I made the cardboard Tardis that had the letter written on the inside – that a little boy had already been on the set of the show. I was devastated, but cheered slightly when my parents bought me a money tin shaped like an old police box, like the Tardis in the *Doctor Who* series was. I was fascinated by technology and loved anything new. My calculator was a good friend and I would never type in an easy sum like one plus one in case it thought I was an idiot.

When I was nine my tiny primary school of 30 kids got a new headmistress, Mrs Knight. I saw her as a second mother. While the previous head had found me disturbed and difficult, Mrs Knight encouraged my talents for writing and drawing and made me feel clever and mature. One day I came into school with a poem I'd written the night before about the Fire of London. Learning about this had affected me deeply as I was terrified of fire. I showed my poem to Mrs Knight and her response seemed inexplicable. She read it a couple of times and went to her office. I thought I'd offended her somehow or that she thought my work was badly written, but she came out of her office in an excited state and told me it was 'marvellous' and that I should be proud. She had probably gone to photocopy it. Mrs Knight seemed to love working with children and had exciting ideas. When there was a general election in Britain she had the class get into groups and design a school logo, then campaign for our group's logo and put it to a vote. The successful logo actually became the official one for the school. We were encouraged to put on plays of our own invention and at school assembly we'd often find that she'd organised a speaker from the village to talk about one thing or another. My favourite was the African lady who told us all about going to school and growing up in Africa. I was fascinated and longed to learn more about other places in the world and meet people from everywhere. Mrs Knight started a book of her favourite poems and stories by children from our school and some of my poetry was published in it. Mrs Knight was fair and even-handed; one time she stood up at lunchtime and said that students had to eat their semolina pudding. After what seemed like forever, a student asked Mrs Knight 'Why don't you eat it?' She never told anyone to eat semolina pudding after that.

I vacillated between being almost unnaturally obedient and incredibly rebellious. My mum likened it to the nursery rhyme of the little girl who had a little curl ('There was a little girl who had a little curl right in the middle of her forehead. And when she was good she was very, very good, and when she was bad she was horrid'). So, while most days I would write poetry and draw and read, occasionally I would do something so naughty it would get the entire school into trouble. One day I stole the key to the sports equipment shed and hid it in a filing cabinet. Maybe I was tired of kids picking on me for my complete lack of sporting ability, maybe there was no reason except a desire to be rebellious. The key was missing for days and eventually Mrs Knight sat the entire school down in the assembly area and told the culprit to come forward. The consequence for the school should I not own up was that there would be no more swimming in the pool for anyone. I sat still and waited with the rest of the school, knowing that nobody else would own up. In the end, weeks later, the school secretary opened a filing cabinet and there was the missing key – right where I had hidden it.

By the time I was seven or eight I'd stopped lashing out physically at other children but I was still definitely a loner. Mrs Knight had made me school librarian, a job I took very seriously indeed. I learned about the Dewey Decimal System and even remember terrorising a slightly simple boy when he accidentally knocked a shelf over. Sports might have solved a few problems had I actually been any good at them or understood the rules, but the few times I played sport with the other kids I only ever earned myself some rude comments and teasing for my lack of ability or my confusion about the rules. Once I played soccer and was delighted to score a goal and puzzled why my team-mates yelled at me. Apparently I'd kicked the ball into the wrong goal and scored for the opposing team.

My brother Dean bought a tape deck with some money he'd saved. We invented a world of characters – 'Sixy' who was 'six maypoles tall' and could eat anything she liked, up to and including bricks and concrete, 'Tapey' who was also tall and practically invincible. There was 'Corcus' who was able to communicate with animals and 'Nigadig' the scientist who mixed chemical cures for various ailments. This world was the focus of our games together for years to come. My mum told me off for mixing my 'chemicals' – coloured water made by pouring water from a jug through a felt-tip pen – and leaving stains all over the windowsill. I would have been 10 or 11. As these characters, we would build elaborate houses of cards (Dean could always make the tallest ones), then see how they would survive aerial bombardment by ball-bearings. Dean would steal treats from the kitchen to hide around the house for me to discover: little morsels of cooking chocolate, fairy cakes from the freezer or cooking walnuts.

As both my parents worked we didn't do many things together as a family, but being mindful of this, my dad planned outings every so often. We'd go swimming or ice-skating. If we were really lucky we'd go to the movies. We also went to that English tradition, the pantomime. I never worked out that the female lead was always played by a man, I thought they just got obnoxious, loud women who wore a lot of make-up to do it.

The only day my parents weren't working hard was Sunday. On Sundays we'd get up early and get dressed in our nicest clothes; I always had to wear a dress. My mum would put a roast in the oven and tie a scarf over her hair. Then we'd drive the ten miles to Cambridge and go to church. When I was young my parents went to the Christadelphian church. Christadelphians are quite a conservative Protestant group who love rules. Everything seems to be set out as a 'can do' or a 'can't do'. I thought other people were evil when I was little: the couple who got a divorce, the girl who swore and 'blasphemed' by exclaiming 'Oh my God!' loudly, people who did drugs. Rather than being prejudiced against these supposedly 'bad' people I tended to feel intimidated by them.

As I got older I started to wish we went to a more mainstream church. I felt that being a Christadelphian only contributed to the fact that I was 'weird', but I still followed all the rules and did what I was supposed to most of the time, trying to enjoy all that being a Christadelphian had to offer. The best Sunday of the year would have to have been Sunday school prize-giving day when all the kids were given a present – usually a Bible or religious book. On prize-giving day they'd have a big party for all the children with party games and food. The adults would put on plays and party acts, which for once had nothing to do with Christianity. My dad was famed for his rendition of the song 'Jake the Peg' (with my extra leg). He kept his spare leg (made with stockings and scrunched-up paper) in the cupboard and Dean and I would beg him to do it again for us at home.

Being a Christadelphian had its disadvantages too. My mum told me there was no such thing as Santa Claus at a very early age, the tooth fairy never came to our house and mentioning the words 'Easter Bunny' would usually prompt a lecture on commercialism and true meaning and so on. When I was ten I had a craving for an Easter egg but my mum refused to buy one so I worked on the farm for as long as it took to earn the money for the egg I wanted. I was envious of people who didn't have to go to church twice on Sundays. We had to go once in the morning for the adults to have communion – known as 'the emblems' – and then in the evening for the 'exhortation', a lecture. Christadelphians are definite fans of academic knowledge and long words. They don't worship in a church but in an *ecclesia*, an ancient Greek word for church. I wished we could sleep in on Sundays and watch TV.

My parents had many friends from church and we'd often go to various people's houses for Sunday lunch. My favourites were the older ones. I'd developed a fascination with old age and thought the

Sundays when we invited older people over for lunch were always fun. I liked 'Sister Wright' who was 88 years old. I worked out that she was almost nine times older than me. She lived in a little house filled with the collected junk of her 88 years. She hadn't been upstairs in many years due to her arthritis but I imagined all the things she'd accumulated over the years up on the second floor. She loved Dean and I but had no idea what children liked to eat – she would give us a can of baked beans telling us, to the hilarity of both our fart-humour-obsessed minds, that they 'were very good for you'. One time she was at our house and walked across the lounge-room emitting a fart with every step and exclaimed 'Ooh, it's very windy today!' This caused me to leave the room and dissolve into fits of giggles that lasted 20 minutes.

I'm told when I was very little I did not realise that 'Grandma and Grandpa' were two separate, distinct people, I simply referred to them both individually as 'Grandma and Grandpa'. They lived in Torquay in Devon, which was a day's drive from our home in Cambridge. I looked forward to going to stay with Grandma and Grandpa more than anything else. They had a grandfather clock, a Purkis family heirloom that some long-dead ancestor had made. Dean and I would get up before the adults and watch this clock until the magical hour of seven o'clock when we were allowed to wake the grandparents and climb in their huge bed. Once Dean and I discussed in very serious tones the 'fact' that 'a watched clock never boils'. Grandma would always make us breakfast in bed, usually boiled eggs with runny yolk and 'soldiers' of toast. Grandpa would lie in bed and ask Dean and me – his 'little coal miners' – how many tons of coal we'd mined from the depths of the covers. Grandpa was a writer and had written a book on the life of Jesus that was famous in Christadelphian circles. His office was a wonderful place filled with strange officey things like a paper weight and desk calendar. Once (I'd left the lounge-room as all the adults were having what I considered a 'boring grown-up conversation') I found a table full of cakes and desserts in the kitchen and guiltily ate a couple of slices of banana from an enormous flan. I thought it couldn't hurt to have another one, and another and another. By the time my grandmother came into the kitchen to see where I was, I'd eaten every single slice on the flan. I stood there, anticipating being yelled at and smacked. My grandma smiled at me and said 'Ooh look. A little fairy has gone and eaten all the bananas from the flan.' When I was ten or so, I borrowed £17, a fortune, to buy a Nintendo game. I was not a prompt payer of debts and this was no exception. Dean had also bought a game for himself and had paid back the entire amount, but I'd only paid back £1.50. I told Grandpa about my apparently desperate financial situation, not wanting to ask for money, rather to let him know how stressful being in debt was. He told me he may be able to help my 'monetary problem', pulled a pound coin from his pocket, and handed it to me. I was so grateful I couldn't think what to say to him.

When I was ten my parents decided to go to Australia for a holiday. The family finances being what they were, Dean and I were told we would have to stay in England with friends. Dean got to stay with a family we knew from church and I was to stay at Agnes's house. Agnes was one of the two women my dad employed on the farm. She was retired but worked a few hours for my dad. I loved staying with her and her husband, Trevor. He was a retired coal miner who spoke in a mumbly voice that most people apparently had a lot of trouble understanding. I was an exception to this rule. I'd always been good at understanding people who spoke indistinctly or with a thick accent and I always knew exactly what Trevor was saying. The thing I noticed most was that Agnes and Trevor never yelled at me (except once when I spoke when the lottery results were being announced) and seemed to love having me around. The weather, however, was an entirely different matter. The winter of 1984, when my parents were on holiday in sunny Australia, was said to be the coldest for 50 years. I disliked the cold, the freezing days and colder nights. Coupled with the fact that my parents had left me behind in this weather while they themselves were enjoying summer, this irritated me beyond belief. I also had to walk about a mile to feed my cat who was staying at my parents' farm. One day, when the maximum temperature was minus eight degrees, I walked up our road to feed the cat and the street was covered in about three inches of ice. I fed Smokey the cat and skidded back to Agnes and Trevor's house. The next day Smokey came to stay with me in Agnes's council flat.

The only drawback to staying with Agnes and Trevor was the chips. As in most working-class English families, chips were on the menu many times a week. Agnes's chips were consistently soggy on the outside and hard in the middle. One night I tripped over the rug and dropped my dinner on the floor. I was greatly relieved that there were no more chips to replace the ones I'd dropped.

When my parents returned from Australia they brought Dean and I presents, all of which were strange and exotic for having come from so far away. I marvelled at the Australian sweets (or 'lollies'), which were like nothing I'd ever eaten before. I loved my comb from a shop in Melbourne's Chinatown, which, while being attractively black and shiny and having a beautiful design of lotus flowers painted on it, was totally useless as a comb. My dad had bought a new camera before they went away and had been buying amateur photography magazines and practising taking photos of anything that moved in front of his lens. Dean and I had teased him about his photography bug and his 'big lens, little lens, 24 millimetre lens'. On holiday in Australia my dad had taken many photographs including a picture of a sign on a farm gate that read 'These once proud bulls can no longer mate, they forgot to shut the bloody gate'. We laughed about this for ages. We thought the pictures of landscapes were amazing. There were also photographs of weird and wonderful creatures at Healesville native animal sanctuary, including a green tree frog that Dean and I were certain was made of plastic and a duck-billed platypus, as well as more commonly known Australian animals such as kangaroos and koalas.

My dad talked about Australia constantly and eventually asked us how we would feel about moving there. My mum was Australian and had similar feelings to me about the English winter. She wanted to go. I also wanted to go but Dean was less enthusiastic. Dean had been at secondary school for over a year now and had made close friends. I, however, didn't have any friends to speak of and had spent the last six months being picked on and teased at school and thought moving to another country would probably solve my problems.

In the meantime I was stuck in Britain. I started at secondary school in September 1985 and from the first day I arrived kids in my own class laughed at me and called me a 'swot' as I was only interested in schoolwork. After a while, anyone who took pity on me and was friendly got picked on themselves and, with few exceptions, usually gave up and joined in the teasing. Older kids would make sexual jokes that I didn't really understand and ask me to hump them, screw them or fuck them, knowing that I had no idea what they were talking about. The only thing at school I looked forward to was Christian club. It was run by Mrs Francis and the kids in the Christian club were often outcasts like myself to some extent and were much nicer to me than most. I also liked the hot chocolate from the drinks machine, which cost 20 pence and was the most delicious hot chocolate I'd ever tasted.

Emily, my nemesis from primary school, started secondary school at the same time as me and became as popular as I was hated. She would amuse her new friends with tales of the embarrassing things I'd done at primary school. I had never truly thought of myself as different until I started high school. In primary school there were only 30 kids and a lot of us were a little different, meaning that some of the things I enjoyed, like talking to the teacher or reading books in the library, did not come under fire from the other children. Talking to the teachers at secondary school was the kind of thing that only made my problems worse, but I had no way of knowing why this was the case. At primary school I hadn't really cared about the other kids or what they thought of me, they usually left me alone. At secondary school most children went out of their way to make my life hard so I began to care an awful lot what people my own age thought.

We waited about six months to find out if we had been accepted to migrate to Australia. My mum, Dean and myself were all allowed to migrate as we were all Australian citizens – my mum having had my brother and me registered with the Australian consulate when we were born. My dad, being English, had to pass all the immigration department's rules and regulations and go to a series of seemingly never-ending interviews. We must have travelled to London ten times for my dad to answer another round of questions. Eventually all that was left was for my dad to have a physical examination. A few weeks later I went to the letter box and found a letter addressed to my dad from the Australian consulate. He had been accepted. We were going to Australia and to a new life. I was going to start again.

2 .

Searching for the Rules

The month before we left for Australia we toured around the UK, visiting friends of the family my parents hadn't seen in years, all of whom became 'aunty' and 'uncle'. Christmas was a huge affair, held at my aunt Margaret's house with all the cousins in attendance. Dean and I received many more presents than ever. I was given a jumper hand-knitted by my aunt with a picture of a cat on it, which I thought I probably wouldn't need in sunny Australia but liked the cat picture. My cousin Sally was very sad that we were going. She was much older than Dean and I and had always loved playing kids' games with us and telling us nursery rhymes. I felt a bit guilty about the Sally situation; Sally had a large collection of sugar cubes collected from various restaurants and cafes she had been to and I'd been steadily eating them when she was out, feeling larger amounts of remorse and guilty pleasure with each one I consumed.

I was getting to talk to all sorts of interesting adult friends of my parents who I'd never met before that I could now impress with my new-found academic knowledge, a new favourite pastime. A French and mathematics teacher who we visited, uncle Fred, spent most of the evening marvelling at my French vocabulary and pronunciation. The

French teacher at my school had said I was the best in my class and I wasn't about to let anyone forget it.

After our month of saying goodbyes, we had to board the plane to Australia. I'd spent my time anticipating a new beginning and a life free of bullying. Nobody in Australia would know me and I had no embarrassing primary school secrets that could be spread around the school. I thought children in Australia would love me for coming from somewhere so different and having an accent. I would be a novelty, a talking point.

The plane journey was horrific; 30 hours of ever-increasing irritation in the company of my family, awful food and the screaming children of other passengers. The ultimate indignity was being sprayed with insecticide by the airline staff on arrival in Sydney to comply with Australian quarantine regulations. The airports we stopped in fascinated me, though. We got to stop in both Bahrain and Singapore.

On the drive through Melbourne to my mum's stepmother Pauline's house I marvelled at the poles the street lights and traffic lights were mounted on. I'd expected it to be unbearably hot, but the sky was cloudy and I thought it was about to rain.

I fell in love with my step-grandmother's house as soon as I walked in the door. It was what in England would be known as a bungalow; a one-storey house, with paintings and tapestries everywhere and a comforting smell. When we walked in the door Pauline greeted us and explained that she was putting the 'doona covers' on the beds. Puzzled, but thinking 'doona' was a wonderful-sounding word, I noticed her putting the quilt covers on the quilts. She showed us a tapestry of her own design she was making on a loom. I thought I'd never met anyone so cultured. I was impressed and a little awed.

Over the next few days Dean and I explored the suburb where Pauline lived and caught the bus to a shopping mall in the next suburb. I thought the South-East Asian people who I saw everywhere seemed beautiful, different and wonderful so I developed a habit of asking as many of them as possible what the time was or where the toilets were. I felt at home in Australia as I never had in England. The air felt somehow 'right' and the people were mostly outgoing and friendly. I warmed to Pauline and her family. Pauline's mum and dad lived in one of the most expensive suburbs in Melbourne. Her dad would proudly show off his lighting system that could, at the flick of a switch, illuminate their entire garden.

We drove in our new second-hand blue car to a town called Wodonga – about four hours' drive from Melbourne. I thought the Australian landscapes were grand and impressive and immediately felt I could enjoy living somewhere as spectacular as this. Dean spent a lot of time complaining that Australia was 'messy' and would happily exclaim 'European trees!' if ever we passed any. I had longed to live somewhere 'exotic' for as long as I could remember – somewhere with colourful birds, hot weather and mountains. Cambridgeshire, where we had lived in England, was flat country. During the trip to our new home we stopped at the side of the road to look at the view and I was awestruck by the endless stretch of trees into the distance, with no cultivated land anywhere in sight.

Wodonga was a small country town in north-east Victoria. Victoria is the second-smallest state in Australia, after Tasmania, and lies in the south-eastern corner of the country. As we drove down the main street I thought it had a rather dismal, industrial feel, with run-down shops and truck stops everywhere and wooden Santa Clauses still lining the streets in mid-January. I thought it did not reflect its surrounds of bush land and farms and hoped that where we lived would be somewhere more homely than the main street was.

My parents had decided to live in Wodonga as there was a government scheme to attract business people to the smaller rural centres. My dad never wanted to live in a city, having been brought up on a farm. My dad had decided to grow flowers for a living so my parents' plan was to rent a house in Wodonga until they could buy a small farm. The government agency responsible for advertising the town to potential newcomers rented us a house in a new estate and we moved in with the few things we'd brought with us on the plane.

I liked our new house. The garden had a huge ironbark gum tree that oozed sticky, oily sap that smelled fantastic. The sky more often than not seemed to be entirely blue – a rarity in England – and the blue was a sharp metallic colour that somehow seemed right. There was a tyre swing on a dodgy rope hanging from the ironbark tree. Our next-door neighbours were a German couple in their fifties, Wilhelm and Uta, who enjoyed inviting us over for cups of coffee. I had unofficial German vocabulary lessons from them, too. The first word I learned was *Vogel* (bird). I thought it was German for magpie, as they were the only birds in our back yard. I loved Wilhelm's thick accent and the way he was excited every time I learned a new German word.

Around the corner there were the Pattersons. Mr Patterson was a policeman. They had a daughter called Samantha who was two years older than me. The first time I met her, she and her brothers were kicking an Australian Rules football. To my horror they kicked it to me, expecting me to pass it back to them. I had no confidence or ability in any kind of sporting activity and had never seen an Australian football before. I kicked the ball as you would a soccer ball and watched, horrified, as it bounced in completely the opposite direction to that which I had meant it to go. Samantha and her brothers laughed and said 'She soccer kicked it!'

Samantha and I struck up a friendship, although our interests could not have been more different; she was 14 and was obsessed with boys, in particular a 17-year-old who lived three streets away, and a singer on a TV show called *Young Talent Time*, Bevan. One day she dragged me along to pursue the 17-year-old, Dominique. We hid in the bushes for what seemed forever and waited in vain for him to come out of the house. Samantha would play her Bryan Adams records and always played the song 'One Night Love Affair' two or three times, telling me it was her and Dominique's song (although I doubt Dominique knew that). One day Samantha turned up in our back yard asking my mum if I was allowed to go to the local 'Blue Light' disco. I was petrified. I'd been to one disco in my life before. It had been held in the local church hall in my village in England and I'd purchased a can of purple hairspray especially. I'd had a miserable night and spent most of the time trying to make out what my classmate, Julie, was saying over the noise. I certainly hadn't danced – as far as I was concerned, if I'd danced I would have been the laughing stock of the whole village. The prospect of going to a disco in a strange country was alarming; I would have to go with a girl I hardly knew and I had a funny accent that most kids I'd met now teased me about. I took my Mum aside and begged her to tell Samantha that I wasn't allowed to go. She did and I was saved.

We had arrived in Wodonga during the school holidays, giving Dean and I a little time to familiarise ourselves with our new home before starting at a new school. We went to the shops in the main street I had been so unimpressed with the first time I had seen it, on a mission to buy school uniforms. When I saw what I was supposed to wear I was horrified. Unlike English school uniforms, which were usually made of dark-coloured fabric, often grey or blue, my new school dress was a green and brown checked thing. It was hideous and, not realising that most Australian school uniforms were of a similar design, I imagined all the kids from neighbouring schools laughing at me in this checked monstrosity. I hoped that I would be less unpopular at my new school than I had been in England.

My school was about a half-hour walk through a park from our house. I grew to dread the last stretch of the trip to school. We did not have a lot of money to spend on clothes at that time and, anyway, I had never had a lot of fashion sense; I didn't mind wearing second-hand clothes from the local charity shop and the few new things I chose were usually unfashionable. There were two older girls who walked the same way to school as Dean and I. Every time we walked past them they would laugh at what I was wearing: 'Oh look, she's got that big coat on again. It's so ugly, but so is she with those big glasses. And where did she get the haircut? Did her mum do it or what?' and so on.

I developed an obsession with clothes. I figured if I wore what everyone else did, the bullies would leave me alone. I longed for limitless money with which to buy whatever was 'in' at the time. I did amass a few fashionable items and had my hair cut at the local salon in what I thought was a trendy style. Try as I might though, I could never get it right and even if I was wearing the clothes that I thought were the most stylish I was still picked on.

I could never work out who was making fun of my accent and who actually thought I was interesting because of it. I would react aggressively to any comment about how I spoke, from boys saying 'Can I have a cuppa tea and a biscuit?' in exaggerated north-of-England tones, to people asking me to 'Talk. I love your accent. Just say anything. It sounds great.' To make myself more 'normal' I began a determined campaign to rid myself of any remaining Englishness. As far as I was concerned my accent had to go, as did any words used in the UK but not in Australia. I was an actress studying for her most important role. I listened carefully to how others around me talked, and learned all the words they used that had a different English equivalent. A pick-up truck became a ute, a flannel turned into a face washer and hair grips were all of a sudden bobby pins. Within a few months I almost sounded Australian, although 't' sounds were an issue because, unlike Australians, my 't' sounds were too crisp. One day I had to give a talk at school assembly about the importance of students picking up litter when assigned to yard duty. Every time I said 'duty' – and there were many – I pronounced it 'dewdy' to the amusement of my brother and probably the assembled students, also.

Recognising people was a problem. I was no longer in a school of 30 children, who were mainly quite easy to distinguish from one another. Now I was in a school of almost 1000. There were two girls in my class who both disliked me and I found them impossible to tell apart. I would call one by the other's name, which probably just served to make me seem more weird to them. I would go to school hoping they were both sick and not there, although if only one of them was there I found it even harder to work out which one it was.

In the absence of any kind of social interaction at school, I immersed myself in books and homework. I enjoyed mathematics, science, English, German and art – everything, in fact, except physical education. Sports at school had always filled me with terror but at least in England the male and female students had been separated, with dance, gymnastics, hockey and netball for the girls and soccer, rugby and cricket for the boys. While this was rather sexist, it suited me a lot better than being expected to hit a cricket ball or, worse still, catch one.

The boys in my new school had plenty of taunts ready for the students, especially the girls, who were not interested in or good at sport. Australians seemed to take sports a lot more seriously than anyone had in England and, while being terrible at physical activities in England had been a lesser one of my problems at school, it became the cause of a lot of stress for me in Australia. Not only did I have to play what I considered 'boys' games' like cricket, soccer and tennis, I discovered that schools in Australia had sports carnivals where children from different schools in the area competed against each other. After I had been to a few of these (usually choosing a sport like table tennis) I began to notice the group of kids who never participated and, nervous as I was, started to talk to some of them.

Sue and Kel were two girls in my year who seemed to dislike sports as much as I did and, like me, were usually picked last when teams were organised. They also bore the brunt of teasing as they were both overweight. They didn't seem all that interested in me, but I was determined to find a friend as I thought having someone to talk to during lunchtime might be more fun than hiding in the library, as I had taken to doing, and may even mean I was teased less. Sue and Kel tolerated me more than anything, but did let me hang around some of the time, even inviting me to their house for lunch when we were supposed to be doing a three-kilometre 'cross-country' run. I found I didn't have much in common with Sue and Kel and they soon lost interest in me.

Dianne was another girl I tried to befriend in my first year of high school. She lived opposite the school in an estate owned by the Housing Commission, the housing provided for low-income families by the government. I'd heard other children talking about people who lived in the Commission flats, saying they were criminals and 'paupers'. Dianne had some kind of intellectual disability and was picked on by the same students who teased me at school. She would invite me to her flat at lunchtime and, although it meant breaking school rules, I usually went. Her mother would barely acknowledge me when I entered and seemed to be from another world entirely. She would always have a drink of some kind on the coffee table in front of her, wine or beer. Dianne's dad was never mentioned and I often wondered what had happened to him, assuming that he was dead as I thought only 'evil' people got divorces and Dianne's family didn't come across as evil. There was never much food in the house and what there was would have horrified my health-conscious mother, but Dianne always shared what there was in the cupboards with me. For my twelfth birthday party, I invited only two people – Dianne and a girl who I'd spoken to twice, Kristy. My mum made a cake decorated to look like a hedgehog with chocolate buttons for spikes. Dianne, Kristy and I slept in my bedroom and at five o'clock in the morning the phone rang. It was a call from my aunty Jean in England to inform us that my grandpa had died. Dianne and Kristy were sympathetic and must have expected me to cry or show grief in some other way but I had to pretend to grieve as I felt nothing from the news, only concern that my friends would think me cold-hearted for not being sad at the loss of my grand-father who I had loved dearly. During my second year of high school, Dianne, her mum and her older brother simply vanished, moving out of their Commission flat.

As my second year of high school approached I decided to change the spelling of my name, thinking that few people liked me due to my having an 'uncool' name. My Jeanette became Janette, maybe because one of Dean's friends used to emphasise the 'Jean' in my name as a way to tease me. My mum told me at about this time that people who don't like their own name do not like themselves.

We had moved from our rented house in Wodonga to a farm about a half-hour's drive from the town in a beautiful valley. My dad became very busy, planting various things and researching different cut-flower crops that would grow on our farm. My mum had also found work in a private radiology practice in town, starting off as a receptionist but planning to retrain for a promotion. Dean and I became used to our parents returning from their respective jobs tired.

I have had phobias of many things for as long as I can remember, but spiders would have to be the worst, closely followed by most other kinds of creepy-crawlies. While still in England my mother had terri-fied me with stories of 'huntsmans', an Australian spider that often grows to the size of a saucer and, while she said they were harmless and 'good to have in your bedroom if you've got a fly', I thought I would probably die of fright if I found something like that in my bedroom. There were other nasties that would periodically crawl out of the woodpile in our lounge-room, such as eight-inch-long centipedes that were reputed to be poisonous and were almost impossible to kill. My mum had to rescue Dean and I from one of these beasts once by cutting it in half with a pair of scissors, after repeated unsuccessful attempts to kill it with insect spray. One year we had a plague of moths that covered the windows so that we were in darkness in the middle of the day, their thousands of wing beats making an eerie noise as they flapped around.

While the children at my school were almost universally unkind to me, there were at least some exceptions. There was, however, not one child on the bus from our farm to school who did not take whatever opportunity they could to be cruel to me. In the entire six years I travelled to school on that bus, there were only two people who ever sat next to me, both of whom were boys. One of them spent the entirety of each journey trying to put his hand up my skirt. My day at school was usually a breeze in comparison to the miserable journey on the bus. In my final year, a boy punched me hard in the face as I was getting off. I have no idea why, but when I went to tell the principal, his friends, seeing my recently-blackened eye, yelled out 'Go Mike Tyson!' I longed for the moment I stepped off the bus and into what I saw as my own world – the world of family and home.

While the abundance of insects and the prospect of the next day's trip to school certainly served to dampen my spirits, for most of the time I was attending high school I enjoyed being at home with my family. Dean and I rarely fought and, even though he sometimes teased me or called me an 'unco' when I couldn't catch or was uncoordinated in some other way, we were friends. Dean was known as 'Pom' at school (an Australian term for someone from England) and I was 'Pom's Sister' and, as I saw it, that was the way things worked. To me, Dean had everything I did not – friends, sporting prowess and academic ability. Dean did not feel this way, as I have later learned, but seeing things from my perspective as a child, he was Mr Success.

Unlike others who I thought were in his position, Dean was actually nice to me. Dean and I played role-playing games whenever we had a free moment. In these games, there is a 'games master' who conducts the proceedings and, of course, this was always Dean's role. We even invented our own versions of these games, turning the police in 'Judge Dredd' into gamblers, or making up new rules to existing games. On our new property my dad built a shed and divided it into three sections, one for him and one each for Dean and I. Dean used his workshop for painting tiny figurines from 'Dungeons and Dragons', orcs, goblins, wizards and so on. He was meticulous and would spend hours at work on a single one, using tiny brushes and huge amounts of patience. My workshop went through many transformations, although I can't honestly say I ever used it for anything. On a home video we made about a year after coming to Australia, I am proudly telling the audience about how I use my workshop for my latest hobby, which is making miniature gardens. I happily show off a mess of soil, pebbles and plant material, which I've slaved over, trying to be careful but completely failing. That was the first and only miniature garden I ever made. Likewise, in its incarnation as an art studio, my workshop only ever saw one drawing produced within its walls. I desperately wanted to be like my image of Dean: careful, tidy, popular, sporty, clever and so on. Dean became the standard by which I judged myself.

When I was 12, my dad came home with a surprise for us. He had bought a shiny new stereo, complete with a CD player. He made us laugh by crouching down and looking into each speaker, feigning amazement at the sounds that emanated from them. The old record player that had come as a wedding present to my parents went to the local garbage tip and we took some time to work out how to use this wonderful new addition to the lounge-room. Dean and I soon discovered a new pastime – listening to the Top 40 countdown on the radio every Friday night. Dean would make elaborate lists of all the songs and who sung them and I would sit back looking at the sliding doors in the darkness and listening to my favourite songs, usually those that fell into the category of 'social comment'. Dean would give my parents a 'favourite song' and stressed that they should follow its progress through the charts. My mum didn't take a lot of interest in this but my dad would often listen to his randomly-allocated song and make comments about the band that sung it. One time he was given a song by 'The Bangles' and commented on seeing the video clip that they were 'sexy'. I looked forward to Friday nights. Not only did they signal the end of another school week, but they also meant another night of listening to *Take 40 Australia* with Dean.

I also looked forward to Sundays and church. On Sunday morning we would all get up early and dress in our nicest clothes, as we had in England. We would pile into the car and drive for an hour to a small town nearby where the Christadelphian service was held in the high school building. Dean and I would go to Sunday school, me hanging around with my new friend Rachael and Dean with his best mate, Dan. We would practise plays and songs or learn about God and his teach-ings. Sometimes we would go into the surrounding bush land and look at trees and rocks, walking through the bush to find tiny orchids or other treasures of nature. When we were older, we had to sit in the meeting room with the adults and watch as they took communion. Rachael and I would discuss baby names for the children we planned to have when we were older and married, and would look up our own names in books to find out if they had a meaning. I was delighted to find that my mum's name, Glenys, means 'valley' in Welsh and Dean's means 'of the valley' and that both my name and my dad's name, John, are different variants of the same one meaning 'beloved of God' in Hebrew.

Our church had more than its fair share of older people. We would have church picnics and outings and I would spend more time talking to the elderly ladies than anyone else. At one picnic a sweet old dear told me that the word 'Pom' is derived from 'pomegranate' and that English people have beautiful skin like pomegranate skin and, while I'd heard several theories as to the origin of my classmates' favourite name for me, hers would have to have been the nicest.

My parents were close to a couple from church, the McDonalds. This family had four daughters, all of whom were older than Dean and I, and lived in a stone house off a dirt track in the town where our church was held. Their house had no front door for about ten years as Mr McDonald had been meaning to re-attach it for all that time but had never got around to it. Three of their girls had found poisonous snakes in their bedrooms at least once and there was usually an enormous huntsman spider sitting at the top of a wall looking down at the family. Most Sundays after church we would go to the McDonalds' house for lunch and plonk ourselves down on the squashy couch to balance a bowl of Mrs McDonald's delicious vegetable soup on our laps.

The McDonalds had a habit of collecting unfortunate animals, including a failed guide dog, a horse with a spine shaped like a 'U' and a goat that broke into the house one time and practically destroyed it. They had, in the time that I lived with my parents, three dogs, a cat, an aviary of birds, a horse and a goat. The McDonalds were very giving and would take in stray people as well as stray animals. Lunch at their house very rarely just included our family and theirs. There was usually at least one person who'd just come down from the country and had no money, or a friend of one of their daughters who'd dropped in. During the first year we arrived in Australia, we were introduced to the Clancys at this house. The Clancys were a family with ten children who lived in a caravan park. They had joined the Christadelphian church, although I have no idea what led them to that church – they were certainly unlike any other Christadelphian family I had encountered. Mr Clancy had been a truck-driver before being involved in an accident, which left him with only one arm and brain damage. His wife was a rough nut, although with a heart of gold. She told us a story once about how her father shot her in the backside for cutting off her sister's hair. The church decided to build the Clancys a house and every couple of weeks a group of well-meaning Christadelphians would travel to their town and work on the building site. My family went there to help with the final stages of the building and to help the Clancys move in. I had to stay in a bedroom with three other children, two of the Clancy kids and the youngest of the McDonald children. I spent a sleepless night sharing a single bed with two others. I wished that I could have escaped having to eat my least favourite vegetable (pumpkin) at dinner and had my own bed for the night.

During my second year of high school I developed a fascination with the Cold War, nuclear weapons and communism. This was possibly fuelled by my interest in science fiction comics and the fact that many of the speakers at the Christadelphian church had a habit of frequently predicting the end of the world. I would watch any movie there was about espionage or nuclear annihilation and read most of the children's books on those subjects and some of the adult ones as well. I'd irritate my family by talking about communism, nuclear bombs or similar things and my essays and stories for English classes were all along the lines of politics or science fiction dealing with such subjects. I was obsessed with Ronald Reagan who was US president at the time and invented a family connection to him. He was, according to me, my great uncle Ron. I was so convincing in telling this story that some people at school actually believed it.

I started to get very anxious about many things and frightened of certain things to the point that I would be unable to sleep. When I was about 14 I thought I was physically unwell as I had constant butterflies in my stomach. My mum took me to the doctor. He could find nothing wrong with me but prescribed medication for nausea. Later in life I had symptoms of anxiety that were identical to my nervous condition when I was a teenager, but the first time they occurred I was sure they were physical symptoms. I became terrified that I would vomit in public and embarrass myself. This of course only served to make me more nervous and thus make me feel worse.

Since early childhood I had been easily frightened by images on the TV and movies and as I got older this became much more pro-nounced. I have always had a phobia about mould and decay and to me the ultimate form of decay was that of a human corpse decompos-ing. Just thinking about this would give me nightmares. One day I was watching TV and a clip from the film *The Killing Fields* was shown. This clip showed the central character falling into a pile of decomposing corpses. I ran from the room, but too late – the image had stuck in my head and I was not about to forget it in a hurry. I didn't sleep for a week. I stayed awake, terrified of falling asleep and dreaming of what I'd seen on the TV. I left the light on all night and prayed endlessly to

God to let me not fall asleep and have a nightmare. After about the third sleepless night my dad asked me if I'd been awake at three o'clock in the morning, to which I replied 'I was studying.' I felt too ashamed of my perceived cowardice to mention the real reason why my light had been on. When I was a teenager, about every six months, I would see something that frightened me so much I could not sleep for days.

Finally, after years of being universally unpopular at high school, I made friends with what I considered a group of fellow misfits. This made life considerably easier for me. I'd made friends with two girls called Karen and a girl in my class who'd come to our school in my second year, Kellie. I thought they were all incredibly cool and felt proud and relieved that they wanted to talk to me. Karen and Karen thought I was funny, even though I could never work out why; I wasn't trying to be funny. Kellie came from a strict Baptist family and her dad was in the army. Kellie would make up characters and draw them. She had a whole little world of these imaginary creatures, much as Dean and I did when we were little. She expected me to be interested in her world, but I found that a bit of a struggle. I liked having someone to talk to at school and to confide in when other children picked on me, but it didn't come naturally to me to care how Kellie felt.

The situation with bullies had always been bad, but as I got older it seemed to get worse. We had a couple of 'integration' kids at our school who'd come from the special school just down the road, Belvoir School. One had Down's Syndrome and the other was autistic. The bullies would say to me 'You're from Belvoir, you're from Belvoir', which was probably less of an insult to me than they thought it should be. I got along with the boy with Down's Syndrome and I thought the autistic boy had an enormous amount of sensitivity and a far superior intellect to most. What upset me more was when they would do things like pulling my underpants down or spitting on the roof above my locker. One day all of my underwear was in the wash, so for the first time in my life I borrowed a pair of knickers from my mum. Unfortunately for me, the meanest bully, Craig, chose that day to lift up my dress in front of all his friends. I had never been more embarrassed and was soon given the nickname 'Granny knickers' by Craig and his mates. Another of their favourite tricks was to break into my locker and steal things. I soon learned to only put my books in there and to take out anything they might like, such as my money or my lunch. I longed to have a quick comeback for their taunts, yet I could never think of one. I also had trouble working out who was being mean to me and who was teasing playfully. If a friend said to me that I was a 'dick head' I'd think it was just as bad as if one of the bullies said it. Bullies also had fun at my expense by telling me outlandish, impossible things that I would believe. When somebody told me the old joke that the word 'gullible' isn't in the dictionary I genuinely believed that it was true.

I got along very well with my teachers. My favourite teachers were my English teacher and the man who took my German class. My English teacher would always give me 'A's for my essays and often came into class with a book for me to read. Once she gave me a novel to look at and I tore the cover off accidentally while putting it in my bag. I rushed out to the shop and bought her a new one. I was my English teacher's favourite student, although I could not see that this probably made me unpopular with the other students in my class. All through high school I prided myself on my consistently impressive report cards. I was surprised if I didn't manage an 'A' for English, German, maths, science, art or home economics. Luckily, my parents never minded that my mark for sport was always a 'C' or 'D', but congratulated me for my prowess in all the other subjects. I found academic tasks as easy as I found social ones hard. I read constantly, enjoying Tolkein, Asimov and Frank Herbert as well as looking at my mum's medical textbooks. I found the workings of the human body intriguing and came top of the class in biology one year, even though I was in a class for the year level above me.

I decided I wanted to study medicine on leaving school. I knew I needed very high marks for my final year, but I figured I was up to it. I had a goal. I was going to be a doctor. My mum had told me that her father discouraged her from studying medicine, as he considered it an inappropriate career choice for a woman, so my mother had studied radiography instead. I decided to do what my mum had been denied. I had started spending hours and hours talking to my mum about anything and everything. She'd listen to anything I said and I considered her extremely wise. I would brush her hair for hours and chat with her, I'd stand in the laundry while she did the ironing and discuss one thing or another. A frequent topic of conversation was the miracle of the individual. I'd always been amazed at the fact that out of millions of sperm, only one had fertilised the ovum that became me. I considered every individual a million-in-one happening and was constantly mind-boggled by the fact that I existed. My mum was happy to have a daughter who respected her so much and had told me years before, when we first came to Australia, that, as her mother had died at an early age, she always wanted her daughter to be her best friend, seeing she had been denied that kind of relationship with her own mother.

I wasn't interested in my dad and saw him as simply being there. He seemed to be constantly clowning around and being funny, but to me that was all he did. Dean's role as the hero had now been usurped by my mother. The male inhabitants of our house mattered less and less to me and I came to see them as being like items of furniture. I started to dread what I considered the unchangeable fact that I would have to marry a man and have children, as I thought was expected of me by my church. I was increasingly disgusted by most things male and the thought of actually having to sleep with one at some future stage was starting to terrify me beyond belief.

Although some of the expectations of my church seemed a little onerous and even illogical, I liked the structure that being a Christadelphian imposed on all walks of life. I liked to know that what I believed was right, to not have to debate morals, as that had apparently already been done. My absolute belief that if I followed the specific set of rules laid down by the church I would be guaranteed a better life in the next world was very comforting for someone as bound by rules as I. To me, God was the ultimate authority figure and I had a direct link to him. I would pray for at least 40 minutes each night before going to bed. God became my friend and confidant. I told him things no one else knew, knowing that he would understand. As my teachers were authority figures I could befriend, to me, so was God. I decided to be baptised into the Christadelphian church. After baptism I would be called 'sister', I would be allowed to take communion with the other adults, I would no longer be a child in the eyes of God even if I was in the eyes of everybody else. I learned all the correct responses to the questions the older 'brothers' of the church asked me. While I knew the rule book backwards, I had little knowledge of the concepts the church elders spoke of: commitment, love, forgiveness, mercy. I tried as hard as I could to feel something about what I was doing, but the closest I came to understanding was to think of myself as a white-board covered in red marks left by my sins and then imagine God wiping the board clean the moment I was baptised. I couldn't think of any really bad sins I'd ever committed, but I'd been told that nobody could live without sinning, so therefore I must have been in need of forgiveness.

The scary thing about being baptised, and something that I was sure God would think was a sin, was that many of the church members gave me devotional books to read or special prayers they had found comforting and I had no desire whatsoever to read any of them. I found these texts completely incomprehensible and could only read a few lines at a time, after which the meaning got lost and confused and I felt I could never understand any of the concepts within them. I was worried that the sisters and brothers who had given me the books would ask me what I thought, but developed a series of pat answers to most queries about my opinions of the things I had been given and felt I'd 'got away with it' when anyone questioned me on them.

After my baptism, which took place in our bathtub, I set about trying to be a good Christian. I had, however, little experience of any kind of redemption so I found this was hard and finally felt that my baptism hadn't changed anything, except that I got to wear a scarf on my head at church and take communion. For a few months I went through the motions of being a dutiful Christadelphian, but it soon became difficult to keep any sense of the rules and my religious fervour was now progressively transferred in an entirely different direction.

Six months after I was baptised, a split developed in our church. The church was plagued with issues that had caused problems for other Christadelphian congregations. Some members wanted the church to be more liberal-minded about who got to participate in services and take communion, while others favoured the more traditional, hard-line approach and wanted only baptised Christadelphians to be included. My world seemed to have broken in two. I had always known what the rules were and that the church I had been raised in, and to which I belonged, knew all the answers. Now there seemed to be no certainties and people who had once respected each other and seemingly agreed on fundamental truths were now arguing with each other. I attended many tense church meetings and began to realise that the Christadelphians, who I had once thought had the answers to everything, were disappointingly as human as everyone else.

My interest in the far left, fostered through my obsession with the Cold War from the previous few years, suddenly became urgent. I watched the news constantly and started seeing political answers to things I had previously explained with Christianity. At the time the Soviet Union collapsed and the Berlin Wall fell I found my calling. I left the church and decided to become a communist.

3 .

Learning Which Way is Left

I was determined to become a communist, even though most people in Australia who belonged to the Communist Party were leaving it in the face of overwhelming evidence that people in socialist countries would prefer a political system similar to Western capitalism. I thought the best way to understand Marxist philosophy was to read Marx himself and set off to the local library in search of *The Communist Manifesto* – one of the two communist texts I'd actually heard of. The librarian politely told me they did not have *The Communist Manifesto* in stock, so I asked if they had Marx's *Das Kapital* and, to my relief, she went and fetched it from the shelf.

While I had read a lot of novels, I had never embarked on reading any work of philosophy, excluding the Bible, and found Marx hard-going. Determined to persevere, I took to reading passages from *Das Kapital* over and over in an effort to grasp their meaning. I also developed a habit of reading Marx everywhere I could in the hope someone would strike up a conversation about my political interests. I read Marx on the school bus, at school, at home and in the park. This had the added bonus, in my view, of making people think I was highly intelligent, although I probably only understood one quarter of what Marx was actually trying to say.

One day a man in the park asked me what I was reading, seeming interested. When I showed him the cover, he excitedly told me he was a Communist Party member and trade unionist and it was 'great to see young people taking an interest in class politics'. Unaware that talking to strange men in the park may not be a good idea for a 15-year-old girl, I took his phone number and that of a friend of his who he said was 'a good union man' and lived in a nearby town. I had never met a real communist before and was very excited. My parents were friends with a Christadelphian family, the Gordons, who lived in the town where the 'good union man' lived, so I arranged a visit. I'd stayed with this family before and had got along well with all of them in the past, although now I was struggling between my memory of them and my new belief that Christadelphians were some of the worst right-wingers around.

When I got to the Gordons' house, I eagerly phoned the number my friend from the park had given me and was answered by an elderly-sounding man. He told me he'd love to meet a young 'comrade' and talk politics and 'Why don't you come along to the pub with me tomorrow morning?' I was so excited! I was to meet a real trade unionist, a true representative of the working class. However, when I told Mrs Gordon where I was to meet my new 'comrade' she was horrified. Mrs Gordon said that under no circumstances was I to meet a strange man in a seedy pub and that I should call him back and arrange somewhere more appropriate. When I called the trade unionist back he was none too impressed and said we could meet outside the tax agent's office in the morning. When Mrs Gordon drove me there the next day he was nowhere to be found.

I continued to read Marx, understanding a little more of it each time I did so, my sense of righteous indignation at the 'bourgeois' upper classes growing steadily with each reading. I needed an outlet for my new political fervour and decided that high school teachers constituted part of the working class and were probably more open to my new beliefs than most of the people I came across, so I started to corner every teacher I could and try to determine where they stood on what I thought were the more crucial political issues in life. Most of the teachers found this extremely irritating and would fob me off, telling me to go away or to 'write it in your essay', but the few more radical members of staff at school took an active interest. I slowly learned about 'the Left' and even attended some teachers' union meetings. I was delighted when the teaching staff walked out on strike over a pay claim and the art teacher painted a spectacular banner in the style of the propaganda banners of the Russian Revolution. I covered my school folder with a red and yellow hammer and sickle and graffitied it with political slogans. I took great pride in walking around the school carrying this folder and hoped students would find it as impressive as I did and maybe even ask me a political question.

Happy as I was to be reading Marx, parading my school folder around and arguing about politics to anyone who stayed long enough to listen, I felt something was missing. I needed to belong to a party, a leftist group who I could discuss my views with and through which I could maybe befriend some like-minded people. I had never heard of any leftist groups apart from the Communist Party of Australia and they were disbanding due to most of their membership deciding to leave in the face of the collapse of Eastern European communism. Not knowing where to start to find a suitable party, I opened the Yellow Pages and looked up 'organisations'. There were many categories of organisation but I eventually found the one I was after – 'organisations, political'. There were about eight listings but only two or three that looked promising. I dialled one of the phone numbers, my heart racing as I waited for the answer. A young man answered and I told him I was looking for a socialist group that 'believed in revolution'. Marx had been very clear on the importance of overthrowing the 'bourgeois' class through a general strike followed by a revolution and I wasn't about to let my new friend Karl Marx down. The young socialist gave me some vague answers, but nothing very exciting, so I gave up and started to resign myself to being the only socialist in our country town of Wodonga.

About a week later, Dean came home from a trip to Melbourne with a present for me, a socialist newspaper he'd picked up from a street stall and thought I might find interesting. Delighted, I started to read it and the more I read, the more I wanted to believe. This paper welcomed the end of Eastern European communism and described the former communist regimes as 'state capitalist'. This paper was exactly what I had wanted – a new rule book. I read it several times over and dialled the number on its editorial page. Another young socialist answered and a long conversation followed. My questions were all answered by someone who had all the answers, as far as I was concerned. I arranged a time to go along to one of the Party's public meetings in Melbourne. I asked my mum if I could stay with one of the comrades for the weekend and she agreed, on the condition that she met the woman I would be staying with and saw what kind of an organisation I was planning to become involved with. A week later we set off on the train for Melbourne and the Party that I hoped to become a member of. We went to a dingy office building on one of the main streets of the city, climbed two flights of stairs and entered a smoky room, the walls of which were covered with posters for protests, public meetings, pickets, strikes and other left-wing events. There were easily 50 people milling around the room, discussing ideas. I had found my party and joined that weekend.

The Party were big on 'making the arguments' to anyone they encountered, much like a Christian group that preaches by door-knocking or singing in the streets. They would sell their newspaper, *The Socialist*, at weekly bookstalls and held frequent public meetings on a wide range of political topics. Every week there would be a branch meeting where different speakers would give a lecture followed by questions and comments from those attending. Protests were popular with the Party, and it did not seem to matter what the cause was. We would attend anything that was even vaguely left-wing and try to convince people attending the protest of the validity of our ideas.

I started travelling to Melbourne once a month to stay with my new-found socialist friends. I would spend the time going to as many meetings, bookstalls and protests as I could and would come home with a box full of newspapers, badges, posters and pamphlets to try to sell to anyone who was interested. At school I now categorised my fellow students based on their political beliefs and tended to consider most of them extremely right-wing. I found a new hobby: selling socialist newspapers to my classmates. Most of them thought this was highly amusing and would pretend to agree with me to get my hopes up, then say they weren't interested. Some seemed genuinely interested at first but then were put off by my fervent attitude and hard-sell approach to politics, while others were openly hostile and said things along the lines of 'the best commie's a dead commie'. This only served to convince me of the fact that I was right about everything and that the 'reactionary right-wingers' would never tolerate a more 'progressive' government.

I was spending more time than ever in the library, mainly to avoid my more persistent critics, but also to corner any bookish students who I thought would be more likely to buy my papers as they were, to me, obviously more intelligent and therefore more open to socialist ideas. One time, I spied one of the few students who regularly bought my paper discussing some political issue with our science teacher. I went up to them and offered my opinion, receiving a firm telling-off from the teacher who thought this extremely rude. I would argue with anyone who cared to listen about topics ranging from Israel's treatment of Palestinians, to Aboriginal land rights and the treachery of the 'class enemy'. I was regularly sent out of my history class for my argumentative comments to the teacher, who I considered an atrocious 'reactionary', and representative of the 'bourgeoisie'. One day, when teaching some aspect of history he thought I would find particularly inflammatory, he sent me off to ask the German teacher whether President Kennedy had said in German 'I am a donut' when he made his famous address at the Berlin Wall, saying 'Ich bin ein Berliner', just to get me out of the way for the duration of the lesson.

At home Dean would listen to my continuous political arguments for a while, then get bored and go to do something else. Sometimes I took this to mean I had won whatever argument we were having, others to think he was closed-minded and stubborn in whatever conservative beliefs I thought he had. When he was particularly annoyed with me he would say to me 'Go back to sleep!', which incensed me. He was also in his final year of high school and had taken classes in politics and economics. He often tried to explain to me some principle of democracy he had learned, or would talk about the laws of supply and demand in economic theory, which I would fiercely denounce as 'capitalist propaganda'.

My mum was exceptionally patient and would listen for hours as I talked incessantly about my political beliefs or complained bitterly about some 'fascist' classmate or another. We would spend what seemed forever in the laundry, she ironing, me talking. While I disagreed with my mother's beliefs, I loved her for listening to me and accepting me. She was the one person in my life, apart from my socialist comrades, that I felt I could talk to about anything.

My dad was another story entirely. My father and I have always been very much alike – we have similar mannerisms, similar reactions to situations and a similar way of thinking. When I was a Christadelphian I had no particular opinions about my dad one way or another and certainly did not find him particularly offensive. Yet the moment I became a socialist I saw him as my opposite and my enemy. I would argue with him vehemently, hating every word he said. I thought him an idiot, a bigot, a homophobe and even once called him 'a waste of space'. As far as I was concerned my dad symbolised and embodied everything I hated in life. One time I was discussing Christianity with him and, in a moment of honesty, told him that there was 'a war going on inside me between the atheist and the Christian'. He replied that 'as long as that battle is going on there is still some hope'. I hated him for this, having wanted him to argue with me and dogmatically try to prove his point. To me, the advice my father gave me constituted a threat. I wanted him to hate me, to think me a fool and react to me in the same way as I did to him. What he did was far worse to my mind; he was being a bigger person than me and I hated it.

Dean and I were both given $100 a month to pay for school books and clothes. It was our parents' idea to give us a sense of responsibility and teach us the value of money. I don't think I bought one item of clothing in the two years I was a socialist and lived at home; I spent every cent I had on my trips to Melbourne. I could afford the train trip once a month and would eagerly await catching up with those I thought my only true friends. I loved the smoky 'centre' where our meetings were held, I loved the company of adults who shared my interest in politics and I loved the fact that, for the first time ever, I was being treated as an adult. Most of the Party members saw children as being capable of making their own decisions and the family as an oppressive component of the capitalist system, so, at the age of 14, I was now considered completely grown-up. I was given wine and beer to drink and even the occasional puff on a joint. I was allowed – even expected – to speak my mind in branch meetings and to discuss our Party views with people I met at bookstalls. The best thing about being with my comrades, though, was the fact that they all accepted me. No one minded that I was 'odd' or different. In a world where the only important thing was politics I was always among friends, providing I adhered to a few simple rules, and if there was one thing I was good at it was following rules.

When my mum took me to Melbourne for my first Party meeting, she was concerned about the kind of people I would be associating with and, as any mother would, wanted to meet them to make sure they were not going to lead me into trouble. Understanding this, the comrades decided I should stay with Tracey, a middle-aged teacher who had been a member of the Party since its beginnings in the 1960s. Tracey was fairly non-threatening by concerned-parent standards and my mum seemed to approve of her. From the moment I met her, I adored Tracey. She soon became my second mother and her flat my home away from home. I came to admire and respect Tracey far more than I did my own mother and wanted more than anything to please her. Tracey smoked, so I started buying the occasional packet of cigarettes, longing to be able to blow the smoke out of my nose as she did. She lived alone in a two-bedroom flat in an inner city suburb, so I thought living alone was sophisticated and exciting. She only drank percolated coffee, so I would complain to my parents about the 'poor quality instant crap' they served at home. Tracey had a new boyfriend every couple of months and I'd heard another comrade suggest that she only went out with men who did not challenge her intellectually. I started thinking that I would like a partner, but I didn't want to leave them after a couple of months, I wanted Tracey to be my lover.

I was obsessed. I imagined myself in her bed, in place of her latest fling, a university lecturer who doted on her and bought her a present every time he came over. I was jealous of her latest boyfriend, thinking Tracey was wasting her charms on this man and would be happier with me. I would spend my month in Wodonga longing for the moment I would get off the train and see Tracey waiting on the platform. I read all the socialist literature she sent home with me and would try to impress her with my knowledge of such things as Trotsky's theory of permanent revolution or the British Party leader's ideas about the Russian Revolution. We would drive through the suburbs to Tracey's flat and walk up the stairs. As soon as she opened her door I would be transported. I was in heaven! Her flat had a unique smell that I associated with everything good. She had a bust of Lenin, a poster of Marx and a collection of every back-issue of the Party's newspaper since about 1970. She would dazzle me with stories from the movement against the Vietnam War and we would discuss political issues late into the night over many glasses of wine.

It was at Tracey's flat that I had my first taste of marijuana. Her boyfriend was over, having bought Tracey a new CD by Australian band Midnight Oil. We had eaten dinner and were discussing the latest issue of the Party's quarterly magazine, *World Socialism*. Tracey opened a drawer in the kitchen and pulled out a bag of something herbal, then set about rolling a thick joint. I was so excited! I'd never been around drugs of any kind, but was very keen to find out what the fuss was about and to flaunt the law. Tracey offered the joint to me, saying 'Don't tell your parents about *this*,' and explained that it was not strong, 'only leaf'. I didn't care what it was, or that it had almost no effect on me. All I cared about was that I was no longer a 'good kid'. I was grown up now, as far as I was concerned, and had committed what I thought was the first seriously rebellious act of my life. I had flaunted the authority of my parents and of that enemy of socialists, the 'State'.

In my mind I was on my way to becoming a real revolutionary, a serious leftist.

As I saw it, authority was split into two forms, the 'good' authority of the Party leadership and the 'bad' authority of my parents, the capitalist class and the 'State', comprising the police, the army and government institutions like social security and so on. I longed to fight against the power of my family and society, but to adhere to the power of the Party leadership. I was living in a dual world. I developed an obsession with the police and now hated them passionately, while at the same time being fascinated with their inner workings and motivations. While I longed to be included in police intelligence files on the activities of socialist groups, I was also terrified of this. I telephoned the Australian Security and Intelligence Organisation demanding to know if they had any information on me, yet refusing to give them my name, my heart pounding all the time I spoke to their confused receptionist. I developed a fascination with terrorists – especially the IRA – and finally made friends with a boy at school. He was also interested in such things and became someone to talk to at lunchtimes and, while other students discussed the latest pop groups and fashions, we talked about making bombs and fighting against the 'State'. I was a little worried about this boy's interests. He seemed fascinated with killing people, which I was not directly interested in, although I realised that would have been the end result of any terrorist actions or a workers' revolution. As a Marxist, I disliked the idea of killing people to achieve political ends, but considered a violent revolution necessary to dispose of the capitalist system. I thought this boy to be a bit of a psychopath, but at least he was someone to eat my lunch with.

I had become secretary of the student council at school, and considered this a vote of confidence by the 'more enlightened' students in my socialist beliefs. I took my position very seriously and attended every meeting. I would type up the minutes of council meetings on our new computer, taking great pride in doing this job well. The president of the student council was a 17-year-old boy. He was a member of the Young Liberals and was politically my archenemy. He would talk at length about his trip to Canberra and the national Parliament where he watched question time and was 'blown away' by the political debate. He discussed the value of the capitalist system, democracy and free trade, much to my disgust. Yet when speaking to this boy I was torn between my view of him as a political moron and the fact that he was actually a very pleasant young man. I found it hard to believe that people with right-wing views could actually be nice, and preferred to think of them all as monsters with no compassion or consideration for others. This meant that most of the adults I had once looked up to and everyone I had known as a Christadelphian now became the enemy.

Having been a socialist for only six months or so, I found myself being very intimidated by views that conflicted with my own, fearing that I would be convinced of the truth of the arguments of someone I disagreed with. I was most challenged by Christadelphian views, as I had grown up with them and had believed them to be absolutely right up until a few months ago. Living in a family of Christadelphians was extremely hard for me and I longed to move out, even though I was now only 15. The worst part of leaving the church was that members would send me letters expressing their sorrow at my 'straying' and offering me words of comfort. To me this was the ultimate insult: not only did my family seem to want me back in the church, people I'd only met a few times were sending me letters trying to convince me to return to the fold. I started to passionately hate Christadelphians and think of them as hypocrites, conservatives and moralists. I went to the school hall where church was held one time and insulted one of the older parishioners who I had liked immensely just the year before. I re-captioned my photo album and any photos of Christadelphians were tagged with 'Chrisso scum'. I saw my parents as having forced me to go to church all my life and thought they had not given me a choice. I would travel to the town where church was held with my parents but stay at my parents' friends the McDonalds' house, making long-distance phone calls to comrades in Melbourne, feeling guilty at the thought of the enormous phone bill that the McDonalds would no doubt receive and then hating myself for feeling guilty about what I thought was a family of conservative Christians.

School was becoming a problem as I was often away in Melbourne on Mondays and Fridays, or skipping classes to smoke behind the church on the school grounds. I also sometimes missed classes as I was crying in the toilets after some particularly vicious bit of teasing from other students. I had lost interest in schoolwork and the only books I wanted to read were published by the Socialist Party and unlikely to be on my book list. I stopped doing homework or studying for exams and my straight 'A' report card was replaced by one featuring a lot more 'C's and 'D's. My ambition to study medicine disappeared along with the marks I needed to realise it. I thought doctors got paid way too much anyway, and that I'd rather work in a factory or supermarket, being at one with the oppressed working class. I had no idea what to do about school and my final year was fast approaching.

On the political front the new president of the USA, George Bush senior, had whipped the Australian left into an oppositional frenzy by talking of a 'New World Order' and threatening war with Iraq. The Party produced any number of newspaper articles denouncing Bush and his 'warmongering', even printing one edition with a front page calling for Australians to support Iraqi dictator Saddam Hussein. On my monthly trip to Melbourne in January 1991 I arrived in that city to the atmosphere of a country at war – US planes had started bombing Baghdad while I was on the train from Wodonga. I spent the first few hours of my weekend in Melbourne at a mass rally against the war. I was caught up in the anti-war movement and thought the war meant the pointless death of civilians. For once there was actually a political issue that ordinary people cared about. Selling socialist newspapers had never been easier. So many people now wanted to know what we were saying about the conflict, although some people still seemed more interested in threatening us for being un-Australian. One elderly man accosted me as I stood on the street corner, papers in hand, and threatened to punch me in the face, claiming protesters had burned Australian flags and assuming I had been one of them. I was terrified, but felt proud to be the victim of a 'reactionary'.

After the huge protest march against the war I went with some comrades to the anti-war vigil outside the American consulate in the

city. The vigil had been there for a few weeks and most of the participants were the kind of people socialists usually avoided – hippies,
'ferals' (Australian environmental protesters in the early 1990s who
were often homeless and heavy drug-users) and some drug-users who
weren't all that interested in protesting but were enjoying the free LSD
a woman with pink hair was handing out to anyone who looked the
part. However, the Party were always on the lookout for potential
recruits and decided to try to convince some vigil participants of the
validity of a Marxist explanation to the issue of the war. I wandered
around the vigil, looking at all the tents from various organisations and
noticing, as time went on, that my Party comrades seemed to have forgotten about me and that I was alone among a crowd of strangers. A
man introduced himself to me as Brian. He was a hippie and spent a
long time describing his recent trip to a peace festival near Sydney. He
was about 35 years old and was very interested in me, asking me about
my political views and beliefs. He also asked me my age, which I did
not consider unusual. Lots of people on the left quizzed me about my
age, as 16-year-old socialists were not all that common. Brian had
some beers, which we drank, chatting all the time. I thought him very
experienced in life and didn't mind talking to him. After we had talked
for a long time, I said I would get some sleep. It was midnight and I was
tired. I wanted to get up early the next day to see what protests were on
and maybe sell some socialist papers to people at the vigil. As I walked
away, Brian walked in front of me and kissed me, the first time I had
been kissed in my life. I didn't like it very much. His face was stubbly
and he tasted of cigarettes, but I thought that was a small price to pay
for my first kiss.

While I had no problem being kissed, I suddenly realised that
Brian did not just want to kiss me. I was terrified. I had to get away but
I didn't know how. He asked me if I wanted to get a motel room, to
which I answered 'No!' He then said, 'We can just do it in a cold,
uncomfortable tent, then.' I told him I couldn't because I had my
period, but he wasn't listening. Completely unaware of what to do,
and in spite of knowing the last thing on earth I wanted to do was
follow Brian into a tent, I walked behind him, into the Campaign

Against Militarism's two-person tent. Brian started to take my clothes off me. I knew we were going to have sex. It was the most horrible experience of my life. It hurt, I felt guilty and the thought 'What would my parents think if they knew?' kept running through my mind. Thinking that being unresponsive would get him off me, I went rigid. Eventually he gave up and went to sleep. I did not sleep, either that night or the next for several days. In the morning, unaware of the fragile state I was in after my night with him, Brian launched into a conversation about Tiger Balm, as if nothing had happened. One of the members of the Campaign Against Militarism laughingly told me she'd had to sleep in someone else's tent because we were in hers 'having fun'. I put a brave smile on my face and nodded. I had never had less fun in my life.

For the next few days I was physically sick – my face swelled up and looked infected and I had a temperature and felt run-down. My comrade and friend Tracey offered to take me to a doctor but I refused, thinking a doctor might discover my guilty secret. The next night I went with comrades Mel and Pete to an arthouse cinema to see an 'R' rated film called *Tie Me Up, Tie Me Down*. The film featured several fairly explicit sex scenes in which the woman was very enthusiastic and plainly enjoying herself. During these scenes I thought to myself 'So people actually enjoy that, do they?'

Brian followed me around for the next couple of days. Everywhere I went, he was too. He turned up at the Party's public meeting on the war, he came in the car with me to a comrade's house. I knew I had to get rid of him. He disgusted me and I was afraid he wanted sex with me again, but I had no idea what to say to put him off. I was trapped, unable to say what I really felt. In the end the Party told him to go away as two schoolgirls from the anti-war campaign had complained to comrades that he had followed them home after a rally. A comrade offered to take him to the house where he lived – a boarding house in an inner suburb. Brian asked me for my address, and, not knowing how to answer any other way, I gave it to him, writing so messily that I knew he would never make it out. Thankfully I never heard from him or saw him again.

On the return trip by train to Wodonga, I met two Aboriginal women and started up a conversation with them. They were a few years older than me and asked me about my sex life – if I'd lost my virginity and what I thought of men. I told them I had lost my virginity, but wasn't really into men and that I was thinking about being a lesbian. They smiled and told me I should do 'whatever makes you feel good, sister'.

When I was about nine, we were driving to church, Dean and I in the back seat talking to each other. I overheard my mum mention a lesbian. Having never heard this word, I asked her what it meant and she informed me a lesbian was a 'woman who loves other women'. I didn't say anything but thought to myself 'That's what I want to be.' I had been attracted to the same sex for as long as I could remember, but it was not until my first disastrous sexual experience with Brian that I actually realised I may be a lesbian. Suddenly I was noticing women and imagining holding somebody soft and curvy and having a girlfriend who would love me like a sister.

I knew I had a problem thinking like this while living with my Christadelphian parents, though. According to Christadelphians, God was very definite on the subject of homosexuality and he definitely didn't like it. Being an honest person, I felt I could not live under my parents' roof and keep the fact that I liked girls a secret. I had no idea how to break the news to them, though, so started up a conversation about gay rights and how same-sex couples should have the same rights and recognition as heterosexuals. My dad made a comment that homosexuality is 'unnatural' and 'weird', to which I replied 'Then I must be unnatural and weird!!' and stormed off to my bedroom. I hardly spoke to my dad for weeks and considered him a bigoted, uncaring Nazi who had no idea of how I felt.

I spent the next few months not knowing who I was or where I stood. I felt guilty that I had slept with a man before I was married and even guiltier that I was a lesbian. While outwardly I held the values of a revolutionary socialist, inside I was my parents' daughter and still held many of the values I had been raised with. This duality caused me to have to justify myself to everyone and left me very defensive and confused. I couldn't accept who I was now or who I used to be, leaving me in identity-limbo. I spent many days crying and feeling either angry at myself for being such a terrible sinner in the eyes of God, or raging at my parents for brainwashing me with their 'religious nonsense'. At this time, one of my Dad's friends from England was visiting. This man had had many problems in his past, most of them revolving around his doomed relationship with his ex-wife. I hated him with a passion and thought him a fascist, sexist pig who had no respect for women or anyone else except himself. I spent most of the time he was at our house arguing with him and letting the poor man know precisely how pathetic I thought him to be. One night I wandered off to the bathroom, took a pair of scissors and cut off all my hair, then followed by shaving off what remained with a razor. I walked out into the lounge-room feeling strangely liberated but anxious at what I knew my parents' reaction would be. My parents and their visitor were horrified, which made me feel at once guilty and angry.

I had enrolled in an art course for my final year of high school after realising I did not want to be a doctor. This course was only offered at the local technical and trade school. I had a batch of new teachers, subjects and classmates and was nervous about how I would be treated by the mainly male students at this school. I had shaved my head in about the third week back, probably confirming my fellow students' suspicion that I was completely deranged. Unfortunately, I'd forgotten that we had school photos the day after I did it. The photographer smiled and remarked that it was 'a bit radical for Wodonga', but the other students treated me as if I were totally mad and made fun of me, one girl writing on the back of my head with a felt-tip pen 'It looks stupid', others staring and laughing.

The 'art students' were considered the weirdos of the school. Most of us had been thought odd at the schools we had come from and I soon made some friends from among my classmates. Violet was an anarchist and had also been at the vigil against the Gulf War, enjoying the free drugs more than the political debate. Her hair was shaved at the back with a purple fringe, hence the name Violet. She was 17 and lived out of home. She'd written 'drop acid, not bombs' on her schoolbag and had a huge collection of strange, dark music. Violet didn't care that the younger students teased her for her hippie clothes and strange hairdo. I thought she was wonderful and wanted to be just like her. We would walk around the school together, discussing politics and drugs, her two favourite subjects, me in awe of her experiences with LSD and wishing I had the guts to 'drop a trip' as she had. Most of the students at my new school were boys doing pre-apprenticeship courses for trades and they considered Violet and I to be weirdos of the worst kind. They would make fun of us and call us names, but Violet didn't seem to care. When I was with her I didn't mind as much, but when I went to catch the bus, alone, I was always terrified. I had taken to wearing a fisherman's cap – fashionable in socialist circles as there is a photo of Russian communist leader Lenin wearing one when he was exiled before the revolution of 1917. A group of boys who caught the same bus as me would take this cap off me and throw it to one another, always keeping it off me until the bus was just about to leave and I would have to run to catch it.

I was enjoying my other school work and of course loved my art subjects. I had classes in painting, drawing, sculpture, photography, graphic design, ceramics, art history and a compulsory English subject. The teacher who took us for painting and art history, Ken, became a role model for me. He was an artist who knew some wellknown figures on the Australian art scene and had travelled to Europe and Asia. I thought him incredibly sophisticated and clever. He told me during a discussion about marijuana that he'd 'smoked too much of it' in his youth and now no longer touched it. Amazed as I was that anyone who'd tried the drug wouldn't want to smoke it any more, I thought he was very cool: how could I not respect a teacher who'd tried drugs? Ken would invite the entire class to his house to watch films – often 'R' rated, controversial ones that none of our parents would have let us watch. From these film nights I developed a love of arthouse cinema. Ken respected me for my socialist views, even if he did not agree with all of them, and thought me very brave for being a gay socialist in our small town of Wodonga.

Initially I enjoyed talking to my Irish-Catholic English teacher, Mrs Murphy. She would bring me the IRA newspaper and I would read it, loving to see the views of those who I thought were oppressed. It became a conspiratorial thing for us, her passing me the paper and trying to look inconspicuous, me grinning as I received this naughty piece of political literature. While we agreed on the question of British troops in Northern Ireland, we had some major differences, which became apparent the day I almost told her I was gay. A girl in my class, Mandy, had been relating in disgusted tones her experience that morning of seeing two women kissing in a cafe. In my fragile state I was upset and angry at her attitude but not confident enough to challenge her on it, so I went to Mrs Murphy, distraught. Instead of comforting me, as I had hoped she would, she proceeded to lecture me about 'immorality' in even more judgemental tones than I would have expected from a Christadelphian. I stopped asking her for the IRA paper after that and only discussed things relating to English classes with her, feeling totally betrayed by her lack of support and not understanding why she felt the way she did.

While in my mind I knew I was a lesbian, I found it very hard to actually tell anyone and each time I almost said it I would be overwhelmed by feelings of guilt and fear. After the incident with Mrs Murphy I was even less able to confide in anyone about my new-found sexuality, although I would happily stand up for anyone else who was gay and could talk about such issues in general terms with no trouble. There was a girl in my class, Sophie, who I had feelings for and thought would make an ideal partner. I wanted to tell her this but had no idea how: she didn't even know I liked women, let alone that I liked her. One day she asked me if I was gay. Not knowing what to say I blushed and said 'Er yeah, I am.' Expecting a barrage of judgement, accusations and disgust I was amazed when she smiled and said 'I thought so.' Incredibly all her friends thought it was OK that I was gay, too. Soon the whole class knew and I felt so much better, not having to keep secrets from people and feeling I was able to truly be myself in front of everyone at school. The girl who had been so revolted at seeing two girls kissing hated me for being gay, as did her fundamentalist Christian friend, but everyone else seemed fine about it. The fundamentalist girl was so intimidated by me that she'd cross the street so as not to have to walk on the same side as me.

I became somewhat obsessed with Sophie, my new love interest, and would think about her most of the time. I imagined her being my girlfriend and thought we must be meant for each other. Sophie did not share my views. She was definitely heterosexual and was not interested in me as a potential partner. Undeterred, I tried to convince her to go out with me, telling her frequently how much she meant to me, how beautiful she was and how I thought about her all the time. I saw love as similar to political argument; you simply needed to convince the other person of the validity of your point and they would give in and agree to go out with you. Sophie patiently explained to me that she was not 'that way' and that she liked me as a friend but nothing more. After a while I gave up, but kept hoping that maybe one day she would change her mind.

Sophie and I were vying for the position of top student in the class, both of us thinking the other was the better one. For the first time in my life I was doing so much school work at home that I had no time for anything else. I put an enormous amount of effort into my art projects and was usually pleased with the results. I would shut myself in my room, put on one of the many tapes I'd copied from Violet and get to work drawing or painting or writing an essay on Salvador Dali, my favourite artist. I was also reading things other than political texts for the first time in over a year. I read one of Andy Warhol's books, Salvador Dali's autobiography and the many novels my teacher Ken lent me. I knew what I wanted to do on leaving school; I was going to put a portfolio together and get into art school. Being an artist was a perfect career choice as far as I could see. Artists got paid very little, spent lots of time reading philosophy and politics and were usually a little different from the 'norm'. I'd fit in perfectly.

After a nervous wait, my results for final year had come out. As my brother Dean had the year before me, I had come top of my school. I set about putting my best artwork aside to take to the many art schools in Melbourne in the hope of being accepted as a student by one of them. I had applied for every conceivable art course there was and felt sure I would get into at least one. After two years of spending all my money on train tickets, socialist literature, marijuana and alcohol, I had no clothes that I could wear to an interview for anything. My mum took me to an alternative clothes shop and bought me a beautiful pair of burgundy jeans and a classy black shirt. At least I had one outfit that looked good. All my other clothes were spattered with paint or were full of holes.

I had 11 interviews lined up at the various art schools in Melbourne. To my disgust, they all clashed with a big protest that all my socialist comrades were going to, a picket of the weapons industry exhibition, AIDEX, in Canberra. For once, listening to the advice of my parents, I decided to forgo the protest and attend my university interviews. I was to stay at comrades Mark and Deanie's house in Richmond, an inner suburb, and mind it for them while the entire household was away protesting. My mum drove me down to Melbourne and I found the key Mark and Deanie had left. I felt no guilt at borrowing a nice shirt in Deanie's wardrobe for my interviews. I felt sure she wouldn't mind, and it was a patchwork shirt in various tie-dyed materials, something I'd wanted for ages and was excited to wear. I felt no shame in borrowing things without their owner's permission or even stealing. When I was little I'd steal money from Mum's purse; as I grew older I graduated to shoplifting and stealing from the membership dues tin at the socialist centre. I felt no guilt whatsoever and thought if something was in the world I had as much right to it as anyone else.

Turning on the news each night was both depressing and exciting. The protest was the first article on most news services as there were frequent clashes with the police and differing opinions of the issues in the media. I saw many of my comrades in violent scuffles with federal police and heard the various ideas put forward about the issues of the arms industry exhibition and the apparent violence of the protesters by different journalists. I so wanted to have gone to the AIDEX picket and regretted having to stay in Melbourne by myself while everyone else seemed to be 'having fun'.

After my first art school interview, I returned to Mark and Deanie's house and tried unsuccessfully to unlock the front door. The key wouldn't turn, so, after much swearing and yelling, I decided to try the back door. When I saw the back door I realised the house had been burgled – the door was hanging off its hinges and there was a trail of papers leading out the door through the back yard. When I entered the house, the TV, video and stereo had gone and the house seemed to have been pulled apart. Torn between calling a comrade or the police, I decided on the latter, knowing Mark and Deanie had insurance and thinking a police report would mean they were paid for the stolen goods. Two police officers arrived, dusted for fingerprints, looked around and asked what had been taken. They informed me that it looked like I had disturbed the burglars and they had left as they heard me trying to unlock the door. I was thoroughly unconcerned by this and not at all frightened. The police officers said they would call a friend for me and get them to take me in for the night, so I didn't have to sleep in a house with no back door. A comrade came over and offered to stay the night with me, but I said she didn't have to and that I would be fine. The next day I rang Mark in Canberra. He had just got back to where he was staying after a number of running battles with the federal police and was none too impressed that I'd called their state counterparts after the break-in. He yelled at me a bit and lectured me about state conspiracies against socialists and the like, leaving me wishing I had not called anyone.

After I returned home I found out that I had not been accepted into any of the art courses I had applied for. I was devastated. My parents had said I could move out when I got into university and this had kept me going for the last six months or so. Having not been accepted by any university, I thought they would say I had to stay with them until I was, and all I had wanted to do all year was move out. Luckily, my mum told me I could move out and they would pay me $100 a week until I got a job. I was to move in February and happily started counting the days.

In early January 1992, US President George Bush senior was coming to Australia and a protest was organised against his visit by most of the far-left. I attended many of the organising meetings for the rally and felt thoroughly involved in the movement. I looked to the anti-Bush protest to be everything I thought the AIDEX one had been and that I had missed out on. I wanted to fight police in the streets, to be on the news and to be as rowdy and angry as I possibly could.

On the day George Bush senior was in Melbourne, a rally of about 1000 people converged outside the Trade Centre where he was giving an address. I felt pumped up and excited. The atmosphere was amazing. There were groups of pro-Bush people and what looked to us like Australian Security and Intelligence Organisation and CIA agents and then all of us leftists wanting to let Bush know that not everyone in Australia wanted him here. The protest was wild and moved along city streets blocking intersections and invading government buildings just for something to do. I had never been so excited in my life. I felt I was challenging the 'bad' authority of the police and government and that I was a true revolutionary. Being a rowdy protester seemed to be what I was made to do. I didn't care so much about the politics by that stage, what I was interested in was the buzz, the thrill and the exhilarating feeling of doing something illegal and apparently getting away with it.

When the protest was over, we all went back to the pub where the Party had some of its meetings. We compared bruises and stories from the crazy day we'd all had. I had challenged a couple of secret agent-looking types who were filming the protest to show me their press cards and they had simply turned their camera on me. Back at the pub, two comrades came up to me and told me they had been approached by undercover federal police officers and had been shown a photo of me and asked where I was. I hid in the pub's toilets as two uniformed cops entered, again with a photo of me. I was torn between sheer terror at whatever unknown fate was in store for me if they found me and exhilaration at being 'wanted', and an enemy of the so-hated capitalist state. I spent that night at the house of one of the more respectable Party members and, on advice from Party leadership, went home to Wodonga until things cooled off a bit in Melbourne. On the train on the way home, I saw my classmate Violet and told her at length of my thrilling, terrifying last few days.

A month later I returned to Melbourne, this time to live. Dean had taken a year off his studies to earn some money working in a factory and we moved out of home on the same day, leaving my parents with just each other's company.

4.

Acting, Independently

I had found a room in a house with a Party comrade, Craig, and a Chinese student, Wei. The rent was $50 a week plus bills and, as I was only being paid $100 a week, I knew I needed to find work. My dad had left me with a little money the day I moved and presented me with a shiny black stereo – a reward for my having come top of my school. The room was large and airy and the house felt homely and comfortable.

I was 17 years old and had never worked, apart from odd jobs on my parents' farm. I was not eligible for any government support and was relying on a weekly cheque from home to pay for everything. I worked out a budget and realised I would have about $3 left after I'd paid for rent, food and bills – enough for a cup of coffee. I needed to find work and find it quickly. I spent the next three weeks going to seemingly endless job interviews, the first one memorable for the amount of embarrassment I suffered when I showed the employer a merit certificate from high school and my school results. Amused, he asked if the interview was my first ever. I wanted to crawl into a hole in the ground and disappear for good.

Every day I would scan the paper for job vacancies and phone all the places that I thought might hire me. I even registered with the social security office to see if they had anything I would be able to do. A comrade, Malcolm, worked at my local social security office and advised me strongly to find a job in case I became what he called 'lumpenised'. Marxists describe the long-term unemployed and career criminals as the 'lumpen proletariat'. Horrified at this prospect I doubled my efforts and eventually found work at a fast food restaurant in the inner city. I was offered 15 hours' work in my first week at the rate of $6.50 an hour. I got paid about $7 more per week than when I relied on my parents for money, but I was delighted. I was so proud to have a job. The work was fairly easy and the obsessive work ethic I'd developed working on my parents' farm meant that I started getting 25 and 30 hours of work most weeks, some of it weekend work, which paid far more than weekday shifts.

As a socialist I was supposed to join a union, yet I was terrified of losing my job and thought that should I start mentioning unions I would soon have very few shifts and be looking for another job. As an unskilled 17-year-old this prospect didn't appeal much to me, so I kept silent on any political issues at work and spent my time trying to impress the manager with my skill and speed at making hamburgers, cleaning and serving customers. I had become a double-person, one part attending every radical political activity there was, denouncing 'the bosses' and selling socialist newspapers, the other following every instruction my manager gave me and being a model employee. I lied to Party members about the union issue, telling them I'd joined the relevant organisation, and I lied to my boss, telling him I needed to swap shifts for 'personal reasons' when I actually intended to go to some protest or another. I became the perfect actress, doing whatever the person I was trying to impress expected of me. I lived in constant dread of being discovered, especially when I was at a protest that attracted media coverage, but I managed to convince most people of whichever role I was playing at any particular time. Once I won the 'worker of the month' award and was unable to tell anyone I knew about it, knowing just how disgusted my socialist friends would be at what they would have seen as my pandering to the wishes of 'the bosses'.

My housemate Craig had decided to visit his girlfriend who was in England so there was a vacancy in my house. I didn't know anybody who needed somewhere to live, but Wei did. Her parents wanted to spend some time in Australia with their children and, as I liked Wei, I could see no problem with her parents living in our house. I offered to teach Wei's parents some English and in return they would cook for me. I looked forward to their arrival and asked Wei to teach me some Chinese vocabulary so I could greet her parents and thank them for offering to cook for me.

Since childhood I have had a knack for languages and found Mandarin a lot easier to learn than Mr and Mrs Tsun seemed to find English. Within a few weeks I was able to converse reasonably fluently in Mandarin and was soon translating for them. They were a little older than my own parents and adopted me as a new daughter, asking me to call them 'Mama' and 'Baba' as if I really were their child. They were both accomplished cooks and enjoyed making delicious Shanghainese dishes for me to try. I soon got used to a proper cooked Shanghainese breakfast with pickled bean curd, rice porridge and spicy preserved vegetables and found this the perfect breakfast to prepare me for the hard day of work ahead. The Tsuns were impressed with my work ethic, but concerned for my well-being, frequently telling me that 'you work too hard'. A few weeks after they moved in I smoked some marijuana and was happily conversing with them in Mandarin. They exclaimed 'She smokes *da ma* and she still remembers her Chinese.' They insisted that I only pay them $10 each week for food and Mr Tsun would cycle for 40 minutes to the Queen Victoria Markets and buy fish, vegetables, fruit and meat for the week's meals. I'm sure they spent a lot more on what I ate than $10 but they refused to take any more than that.

Mrs Tsun was both a Western and a Chinese doctor and wished to start up a pressure-point massage business. She would give me a massage most nights, for any medical problems I might have or just for relaxation. She was a master at what she did and one time gave my mum a pressure-point massage for her bad knees, which my mum claimed alleviated the problem for two years. I became the translator for Mrs Tsun during her massage sessions, having to try not to be embarrassed by her clients telling me their various ailments and relaying them to Mrs Tsun in Chinese. Sometimes I found it hard not to dissolve into giggles, especially when I had to explain the difference between the words 'peanuts' and 'penis' in front of one bemused client.

Life with the Tsuns was usually very enjoyable; I liked having them as company and the beautiful Chinese food that was cooked for me each day was an added bonus. The only problem I experienced in the household was Jack. Jack was a 40-year-old waiter at a local Chinese restaurant who came around most nights with leftovers from his workplace. He had quite a crush on me and his attentions caused me an endless amount of anxiety. I had come across many men who found me attractive and it was my biggest worry. I never knew how to get rid of them. I was too guilty and shy to tell them I was gay – a response that deters most men – and I was unable to say 'no'. I spent many hours trying to discourage Jack without actually being able to tell him I wasn't interested. As far as he was concerned I was probably leading him on, or at least sending mixed messages, and he became more and more persistent. When he asked me to marry him and move to China I felt so trapped I thought I would die. Luckily for me Mr Tsun could see that I wasn't interested and asked Jack to stop coming over and to leave me alone. He never came to our house again and I was so grateful I could have cried.

I had started learning the martial art Aikido, on the advice of an older comrade who practised it himself, Mick. I had met Mick when I still lived at home and respected him perhaps more than anyone else I knew – he was intelligent and very confident. He would talk at length about something or another he was interested in. Mick was a black-belt in Aikido and was passionate about his sport. I became enthused and, as soon as I settled in to my home in Melbourne, went along to the nearest Aikido club. I enjoyed the physicality of the sport and the fact that it involved what I saw as aggression, yet channelled it into an acceptable form. Aikido is a non-competitive martial art, so the fact that I wasn't particularly proficient at it was not a problem and other members of the club were supportive and encouraging. The founder of

Aikido was a Japanese master called 'O Sensei' and all clubs have a photograph of him displayed. I decided to name my new kitten Sensei.

I began spending a lot of time with Mick and helped him learn some Chinese. I would catch the train to the outer suburb where he lived and spend the afternoon listening to his 1960s CDs, drawing him nude (he frequently offered his services as a life-model) or discussing union politics with him and his wife, who was not a socialist, but held left-wing views and had a keen sense for the internal workings of trade unions. Mick took it upon himself to be my tutor in all aspects of life and obviously enjoyed having someone like me who hung on his every word. I thought he could do no wrong and felt privileged that he was sharing his many insights with me. I did think him a bit of a know-it-all but thought he had good reason to be, having lived such a fascinating life. He would talk at length about one of his ex-girlfriends who he claimed was profoundly psychic, could see ghosts and communicate with their cat. In fact, Mick was fascinated by anything paranormal and when his wife was expecting their first child he was quite worried about what he would do should the child be psychic and possess what Mick called 'The Shining'. Once again I had found an authority figure, a surrogate father with 'good' politics, rather than my actual father who I considered substandard in most respects.

I did not know 'the rules' when it came to things like sex and relationships. In fact I was almost completely unaware of what constituted flirting and would often find myself with some older man asking me to go out with him or even to go home with him before I'd realised he was interested in me. I didn't know the rules about looking at people, either. One time a gay workmate had to make up the excuse that I was going out with him because a very pretty girl had caught me staring at her legs in the changing room at work and had accused me of being 'one of those lesbians'. I was unaware that I'd even looked in her direction, and was probably looking at an object behind her or a logo on her clothes. She was not the kind of girl I was attracted to, yet to her I was a pervert. My manager had realised he was onto a good thing with me too, as I would take any shift I was offered, even if it meant I had no days off for months. I was terrified of losing my job and thought if I refused to work a shift even once I would lose my job. I had an impressive amount of money saved after having worked for only six months but I had no time to myself and was beginning to dread the telephone ringing as I knew it would probably be my boss calling me in to work.

I was now determined to get into art school and decided to work on a portfolio independently, having heard that most art colleges were more likely to accept candidates who had some experience of life outside of high school. I befriended a couple from the Socialist Party who were artists, George and Julie. George was a painter who had recently graduated from the painting school at Melbourne's Monash University. George and Julie lived in the same suburb as me – about 15 minutes' walk from my house – and rented a two-bedroom house filled with trinkets, artworks and oddities. They had a rabbit, a chicken and a dog and a huge collection of books and music. They became the first friends near my own age I'd ever really taken an interest in. About three weeks after I started my fast food job, I spent $25, a fortune for me at the time, on an Indian doll from my favourite alternative clothes shop in the city and wrapped it up for George and Julie as a gift. They refused to accept it on the grounds that it was too nice to give away and had cost a large percentage of my meagre wage, so it stayed in my bedroom and became the subject of many drawings from then onwards. George showed me how to use his etching press and we made some prints together. He was quite scathing of my first attempts, but, determined to become an artist, just like George, I persevered. George would take me out late at night to various locations around Melbourne to draw buildings and industrial sites. I so wanted to paint and draw just like he did and started to compare my works to his, trying to infuse mine with the same gloomy atmosphere of his canvases. We had many adventures driving around in his car, looking for the ideal subject. One night we started drawing outside what we thought to be a deserted shop at about 2 am, talking and laughing loudly, thinking nobody could live in the bleak industrial area where we were. After we had drawn there for about an hour, the door creaked open and an old woman in dressing-gown and slippers looked out at us and started to yell at us about the noise we were making. George and

I jumped up and ran for the car, our hearts pounding, us laughing about the experience for weeks afterwards.

George and Julie had music by people I had never heard of: Nico, Leonard Cohen, The Velvet Underground, Josephine Baker. They also had any number of books by strange authors such as Anais Nin, Anthony Burgess and Philip Roth. I read their books as fast as they could lend them to me and taped most of their music for myself. George had acquired most of his large collection of art books through illegal means. He was an accomplished thief and had no qualms about shoving hardcovers down his trousers and walking out of the shop. He related gleefully the time he and a friend from art school had smashed a vending machine at college and spent the night eating chocolates. I had no problem accepting George's theft, as I had stolen throughout my life and, as a socialist, thought property immoral, anyway. After having been caught shoplifting only a year or so previously I myself had no 'nerve' and was completely unable to participate in George's outings to the book shop or the art supplies store to 'load up'.

In the first few months of our friendship, George and Julie would happily invite me over to their place and we would chat for hours. After about six months, though, I started to notice them being a lot less enthusiastic about my visits and would frequently be told they were 'just on their way out' when I called. Trusting and naive as I was, even I couldn't deny that they were fobbing me off. My suspicions were confirmed when they informed me that if they didn't want to talk to someone they'd tell them they were just on their way out. I started to call them much less frequently and hardly go over to their house at all.

I was beginning to need somewhere to go after work as Wei's parents had gone back to China and Wei herself had moved out and was living with her new boyfriend Sam. Sam and I had disliked each other from the first day we met and I didn't bother trying to be polite about the fact that I thought him spineless, pathetic and dull. Wei had given me the number for his house, but I never called it, fearing he would answer and we would argue. All the time I spent at home was with myself for company and I was incredibly lonely. I had about three people I regularly called, but the hours I worked meant I was usually at home when everyone I knew was at work. I had about $1500 in the bank that I'd saved since starting work, but I had nobody to go out with and spend it. I would sit on the floor in the hallway of my house by the phone, waiting for it to ring, or fruitlessly trying the numbers of the few people that I knew. My only social outings were to the weekly socialist branch meeting and to the Party bookstall, but I had little to say to my comrades apart from political discussion and I was becoming disillusioned with the Party leadership, so political discussions often became political arguments.

A few weeks after Wei moved out, our landlord informed us that I would also have to move out, so that his son could move into our house. I was engrossed in my second attempt at gaining entry to art school and had produced what I thought was a reasonable portfolio of paintings and drawings. George had told me he thought I would get in 'easily'. He had given me some pointers about what to say and what not to say, so I was feeling quite confident about my prospects. After three interviews and a nervous wait of a couple of weeks I got my first letter from the Victorian College of the Arts, a prestigious school every applicant seemed to want to get into. I had been unsuccessful. It was the final straw as far as I was concerned. I lost any hope I had for the remaining two schools and thought I would be making hamburgers for the rest of my life. When I called Julie and told her, she came over to cheer me up. I was short with Julie, insulting her without knowing what I was saying and before long she had stormed off, claiming I was 'a loony'. I lay on my bed and cried, thinking my situation could not get much worse.

A week later a second letter arrived, this time from the Royal Melbourne Institute of Technology (known as RMIT), an art school with a good reputation. I didn't want to open the thing and left it on the table for some time, not wanting to know what it contained. Finally I found the courage to open it and was amazed to see that I had been accepted. I was going to be an art student and a painter like George. Thrilled, I called George, who congratulated me and then spent some time telling me about the head of the painting department and how he was a right-winger and 'a moron'. I didn't care if the head of department was a moron, and he could have voted for the most right-wing party in the world. Nothing was going to bother me ever again as far as I was concerned.

My living situation was problematic, as the time we had to move out was fast approaching and I had nowhere to go. I looked for share-houses in the Saturday paper and went to several interviews with no success. Everybody seemed to want a 'professional' and working at a burger restaurant didn't really qualify me as a professional. The fact that I was about to start full-time study also tended to put people off, as did my age. The only people that seemed to want me to move in were sleazy, middle-aged men who placed adverts along the lines of 'young woman to share with older professional man'. The only place that I considered moving into and whose occupants wanted me was a house-hold of older lesbians, but I found them all quite intimidating and worried about what would be expected of me if I moved in. I was getting desperate, going to as many house interviews as I could between my many shifts at work, but finally I found a room. It was in a house in Richmond, an inner-city suburb of Melbourne. I was a little bothered by the man who interviewed me, Keith. He said he was 40 but looked more like 32. He came across as someone with a past, but I was rapidly running out of time to find a place so I agreed to move in with him and his three other housemates.

The week before I moved into my new room in Richmond I was robbed. I had been cleaning our house for the real estate agent's inspection and two rather scary-looking people had arrived at the front door, claiming to be looking at the house. While I showed one of them around the lounge-room and kitchen, the other stole my wallet from my bedroom. I did not realise for several hours, enough time for the thieves to forge my signature and withdraw $1300, a huge per-centage of my savings. I was convinced Wei, who had dropped by earlier to help with the cleaning, had stolen my money and therefore had no problems with helping myself to all her oil paints and her cat carrier. A couple of days after I moved into my new room, I called her and accused her of stealing my money, even though it was far more likely that the two people inspecting the house had done it. She right-fully accused me of stealing her paint and we never spoke again.

Life at my new share-house was very different from life at Wei's. Keith was a prolific dope smoker and frequently offered me joints and bongs to smoke. I enjoyed his company and the free drugs but found him incredibly disrespectful to women and quite racist, even though his mother was Asian. Terrified of what he might think of me should I challenge him I held my tongue when he said anything that offended me and never told him that I was gay or a socialist. I suspected that Keith was sleeping with the two other women who lived in our house and before long I realised that he wanted to make me his third live-in girlfriend. As before, when faced with the prospect of an unwanted relationship with a man, I had no idea what to do to escape from the situation and found myself being drawn in deeper and deeper. Keith never actually touched me without my permission but he would often make crude sexual remarks about me or ask about my sex life, and even tried to kiss me a few times. He was also a complete neat-freak and didn't cope with mess of any kind. He claimed this was due to the three years he'd spent in the cramped conditions of a prison cell, serving time for drug trafficking some years previously. One day I came home from work to find him stressing out about one cornflake I'd acciden-tally left on the kitchen bench at breakfast. He angrily told me to 'clean it up', and I wondered why he hadn't just tossed it in the bin himself.

I had started at RMIT as a first-year painting student. I seemed to be the only person who knew nobody else, and was too shy to speak to anyone. I also had a feeling that all the other students would be far superior artists to me and found them intimidating, even before I had seen any of their work. It took me weeks to pluck up the courage to speak to anyone in my class, but eventually I started talking to a woman named Sharon. Sharon was a few years older than me and had a face that reminded me of paintings I had seen of the Virgin Mary. I was correct in thinking she was good to talk to and soon was spending lots of time with her and her two friends. She laughed in shock and surprise when she introduced me to her boyfriend who was in the year above us and I remarked, after looking him up and down, 'So this is your *Man* is it?' I was unaware there was anything strange about my reaction to her boyfriend, but felt embarrassed as I'd obviously said something rude and offensive. Sharon's 'Man' and I soon became friends and he found my apparent rudeness quite funny. Sharon and her boyfriend lived very close to RMIT and I soon moved in very close to them, having found Keith's advances and sexism too much to bear. I was now living with Jose and Gerard, two brothers who were also fellow socialists.

Jose and Gerard were two of the most unique individuals I had ever met and I thought living with them would be so much more enjoyable than sharing a house with a male chauvinist who spent most of the time making sexual comments and smoking drugs. When I moved into my tiny room in the brothers' three-bedroom house, they informed me their cat had christened the room by using the floor as a toilet – her way of greeting a newcomer. I was delighted, as I knew I would no longer be worrying about leaving cornflakes on the bench or about mess of any kind. Jose and Gerard were certainly not neat-freaks and that suited me just fine.

At work the new manager had thought me an excellent choice to work the two all-night shifts on Friday and Saturday nights. I had accepted this unquestioningly, thinking of the money I would be paid for all this extra work and being too afraid of losing my job to say no. I would come home from art school on a Friday afternoon, have a cup of tea and try to get a couple of hours' sleep. Then, after a fruitless attempt to sleep, I would get up at 10 pm, tired and grumpy, and walk into the city to start my ten-hour night shift. On Saturday I would come home and sleep all day, then get up at 10 pm and go to work again for 11 hours. Sunday would be a write-off and on Monday I would go to my painting class at RMIT and then do an evening shift until 11 pm that night. Basically I had no time for a social life of any kind and was even told by my boss to 'sober up and come to work' when he called me in on the one occasion I dared to go out with Jose's friends for lunchtime beers at the local pub.

A far greater problem soon arose at work with the new boss. He was a married man with two children, but decided he wanted to 'fool around' with me on my breaks at work. I was terrified of this boss and even if I'd had the courage to stand up to him, I would not have known what to say to put him off. He would call me to the back room at least twice a day and kiss me, touch me and once tried to have sex with me. That time I was fortunately saved by the phone ringing in his office. Once again I was faced with a situation I was not equipped to deal with. I told my mum on one of our rare telephone conversations that my boss was harassing me and confided in her that I'd thought about calling his wife and telling her. My mum said his wife would just hate me, and, not wanting to cause myself any more trouble, I decided maybe that was not the ideal course of action. I tried telling the boss that I didn't want to 'play' but he grinned at me and said 'You know you like it.' I could see no way out, so, after working at my job for two years and having been promoted to junior manager, I quit without asking for a reference or severance pay. I felt as if a weight had been lifted from my chest. I was free! My heart no longer sank when the phone rang: it could not be my boss calling me in for a shift. I no longer had to be outwardly happy and polite when inside everything was black and churning. I applied for a student grant and shaved my head. I was going to do and be whatever I wanted to from then on.

Being able to devote myself full-time to my painting course was great. Not having to work two night shifts and four or five day shifts a week left me with so much free time it was magical. I could go to the pub to see bands, or just drink beer. And with over $4000 in the bank, saved from working almost every day for the last two years, I could afford to smoke marijuana a couple of times a week. I would walk the 20 minutes to my art course at RMIT, past the Queen Victoria markets, and smile, with the sun shining on my face and the smells of the market drifting by. I'd smile at everyone I saw, not caring what they thought. When I got to RMIT I'd take the steps up to my studio two at a time, just happy to be able to do so.

As a Marxist I had several philosophical views that conflicted with the kinds of ideas being taught by my tutors and I took this to mean that my tutors were my enemies and that I should not listen to what they said. One morning I got in bright and early and argued with the head of first year painting for an hour, telling him exactly what I thought of him in no uncertain terms. My classmates all assumed I was under the influence of marijuana or alcohol, but I was completely sober. I had nicknames for all my tutors and none of them were very nice. They all tried to be patient with me, but I would not listen to a word they said and thought them all participants in some right-wing, anti-Marxist conspiracy. I also graded my fellow students according to what I considered their artistic merit to be and only talked to those who I thought were below-average, as I saw myself to be. One student, who I considered to be the best painter in the entire class, offered to swap one of her magnificent paintings for a small picture I had made. I thought her totally mad and told her so, refusing to part with my painting because I thought she was getting by far the worse end of the deal. Most of the people I talked to were those who painted, as I did. For some reason I thought anyone who made sculptural, photographic or installation-based art was in a different league to me and that I was not worthy to speak to such people.

By the end of first year I had a reputation as a 'wild child' and most other students assumed I had tried hard drugs and that I was stoned for much of the time. In fact I rarely smoked marijuana, drank alcohol even less frequently and had never touched anything harder than beer or dope. I didn't mind people thinking I was a bit of a delinquent as it was the perfect excuse for my strange behaviour and, unlike at high school, I was respected for being different, even admired by some. I didn't listen to a word any of my lecturers said to me and my painting style remained pretty much the same for the whole time I was at RMIT, despite the many efforts by my lecturers to challenge me and to inspire me to try something different. I thought I was not very good at painting, but it was the only medium I knew anything about and I was terrified to try my hand at anything else, in case I was even worse at that. Lecturers would question me as to why I just painted and I would change the subject to something less challenging. My marks consistently hovered around 60 per cent and I was unaware that they gave out marks over 80 per cent, that grade having eluded me throughout my studies.

I started to spend a lot of time in the company of a fellow first-year student, Anand. He was aloof and strange. Anand was brought up in a conservative Northern Indian family and would complain bitterly about his parents to anyone who would listen. He smoked a lot of marijuana but seemed stoned even when he was not. He was softly spoken and had an affected British accent. I suspected that his strangeness was partially an act put on to make him seem more interesting, but I enjoyed his company, even if I found him a little frustrating at times. He'd ramble on endlessly about the light in the trees or the pattern of the coffee in the cup and seemed to be acting out his image of what an artist should be. We would draw each other nude or sit in the cafes sketching all the customers, not caring what they thought. Anand seemed to know everyone in Melbourne and someone would greet him almost every time he walked down the street. He would bring dead birds and spiders into the studio to sketch and didn't seem to care when he was asked to dispose of them by the health-conscious lecturers. Other students thought that we were more than friends, but the only intimate moments we shared were those we had while drawing each other in the nude. I found it convenient to have a pretend boyfriend. I could tell any men who were interested that I was going out with Anand and they would leave me alone. I'm not sure what Anand himself thought of the arrangement but he never complained about spending time with me and did not try to touch me even once. We must have made a strange couple, him talking dreamily of patterns of light and the art that he saw in everything, me defensively arguing politics with anyone I disagreed with.

In 1992 the people in my home state of Victoria elected a new state government and leader, a man called Jeff Kennett who was public enemy number one as far as the Socialist Party and most other left-wing groups were concerned. Kennett's policies were beneficial to the economy but we on the left considered them hugely detrimental to the social good. Schools were closed, government employees sacked, local councils were disbanded and money channelled into big projects such as the building of a casino and campaigning for the Australian Formula One Grand Prix to be held in Melbourne. To the left this meant war.

We thought Kennett had upped the stakes and we weren't about to let him get away with any of it. Protests were organised and socialist newspapers were printed running editorial after editorial against 'Jeff'. I attended the biggest rally I'd ever been to, a general strike and march through the streets of Melbourne attended by almost 100,000 people. I thought the people were about to fight back, as the Party had been predicting since I joined, and I wanted a piece of the action.

For my fellow leftists, being involved in political action was about stopping a school from being closed, or standing on a picket line alongside wrongfully dismissed workers. There was an emotional involvement for the average socialist; he or she *felt bad* when a perceived injustice was committed. Socialists and others on the left are often described as having a 'social conscience' and to most it's exactly that. Yet I had joined the left as a sort of substitute to the set of rules I had grown up with. I constantly tried to feel something for those I was defending, yet I couldn't.

Feeling may have been beyond me, but fighting wasn't. When I first joined the Party the only kind of fights I had were verbal ones: arguments with my parents, or someone at school, or a church member. However, by 1992 I had been involved in some physical fights for political causes, too. I had engaged in fights with the police at protests or with right-wing protesters at a march organised against the neo-Nazi skinheads. The only times I felt anything about my political beliefs was during these physical confrontations, when my heart was racing and each moment mattered. By the end of 1993 I only ever felt good when I was stoned or when I was attacking police officers at some protest or another. I lived for the adrenaline rush of what we socialists termed a 'militant' protest; in other words, a protest where things got rough. I had no idea of right and wrong when it came to these protests. To me the police deserved my violence and it 'wasn't like I was going to kill them or anything'. My morals were based solely on following rules and, as far as I was concerned, I wasn't breaking any of them. I was following the socialist rule book and in that rule book there's nothing wrong with physically attacking the police – they constitute 'the enemy'.

Fascinated with the dark side of society, with prisons and criminality, drug use, terrorism and anything else that disrupted the order of society's workings, I wanted to be hated by the police, to be an 'enemy of the state'. I set about becoming that in every way I could. At the end of 1993, just before I left my fast food job, I attended a picket line at a secondary school that had been closed by the Kennett state government. At this picket the police had been somewhat overzealous in their treatment of the predominantly peaceful protest and had attacked the picketers brutally with batons. The next day I set off for the picket line, which had received world-wide media attention for the violence the previous day. I was determined to incite the police in whatever way I could. I ended up being arrested that day, along with seven other picketers. Unlike the other seven, who found the experience very frightening and unpleasant, I was enthralled by the processes at work and the structure of the police force and came away from the day feeling excited and invigorated. I attended the meetings of the 'Richmond Eight' as we became known and, while the others were concerned about the consequences of having been arrested at such a high-profile protest and the upcoming criminal court case, I felt more alive than I ever had before. I treasured the forms I had been given by the police on the day of my arrest and would frequently take them out and read all that was written on them.

Two months later there was another protest. This time the aggression was largely instigated by the mostly socialist and anarchist protesters and I was in the front lines the entire time. Towards the end of the march, which by that time had become a scuffle outside a club frequented by the very rich, I realised that I had escaped the attention of the police even though I had been provoking them the whole time. As the protest disbanded I ran up to the police line and knocked the hats off two officers, who grabbed me and threw me into the waiting police van. Once again I was off to police headquarters with my heart racing and a strange feeling of contentment spreading through me. I was at once excited and terrified, hooked on the rush of the fight, not caring what the consequences may be.

One month after my second arrest, two police officers knocked on the door of the house I was sharing with Jose and Gerard, asking for me. They informed me that I was required to answer questions about some video evidence they had from the last protest. Suddenly I understood some of what I was involved in. They wanted to charge me with assaulting police. This charge could carry a prison term and indeed had in the past for some protesters. I spent weeks in a state of sheer terror, wondering what was going to happen to me. I started to only think about my court case and the possible consequences, feeling anxious most of the time. Then, after a month or so, I would joke about how I was 'going to jail. Ah well, not much you can do is there?' to all my friends and soon was living my fantasy of being the enemy of the state. I was possibly going to be a political prisoner. There would be posters featuring my photo and 'Free Jeanette Purkis' emblazoned across them. People would graffiti the streets with political slogans suggesting my imprisonment was an act of a 'Victorian Police State'. Instead of worrying about going to prison I started to look forward to the unknown, but no doubt noble, acts that lay before me as a prisoner of the capitalist state.

Some Party comrades were beginning to see me as slightly mad and obsessive. I had been lectured by one woman so many times about being what she called 'ultraleft' that I started avoiding her at meetings. I was not all that interested in discussing politics any more and only went to bookstalls and branch meetings because I thought it was expected of me. My obsession with the 'darker' side of life and authority was becoming my whole world.

5 .

Becoming the Enemy

I had moved yet again, this time moving in with an anarchist and a feminist I knew from the school picket at which I had been arrested, Sam and Evie. Sam and Evie were a couple and were out most of the time so I didn't have a lot to do with them, apart from in the evenings when we would smoke marijuana together and discuss our days. I was in my second year at RMIT and not enjoying my studies very much, spending more time thinking about my various police charges and hoping for another violent protest at which I could misbehave some more. I wasn't going to classes much and was very rarely in my studio. I was also stoned a lot of the time and so had little motivation to do much other than chat with friends or watch arthouse movies alone in the Kino cinema.

I had been desperate to have a girlfriend for as long as I had known I was a lesbian, yet I had had no luck with women at all. Men seemed to universally find me attractive, much to my dismay, but no woman had yet shown an interest in me. I had kissed a couple of girls before at feminist marches and once at a gay kiss-in at a protest, but I'd never gone further than that. I was so impatient, but not confident enough to ask anyone out that I liked, thinking they would be bound to reject me.

When I had lived at Sam and Evie's for about three days my old housemate Jose came over with his girlfriend Jo and another girl who I knew from the Party, Carol. Carol was two years younger than me and still at high school. I thought she was quite plain-looking but enjoyed her company. That night we all chatted and drank beer 'til about midnight and, as we were going to bed, Carol asked if I wanted to go out with her. Without hesitation and having given no thought whatso-ever to the possibility of a relationship I eagerly replied that yes, I liked her too and would love to go out with her. We went to my bedroom, me thinking all this relationship stuff must be about sex and happily stripping off. Poor Carol asked if I wanted to talk before we did the deed. I knew I had done something wrong once again and was a little discouraged, thinking I'd much rather have sex with Carol than talk to her.

Carol and I were soon spending most of our free time talking on the phone or lying together in my bed. I was so happy. Someone actually liked me *that way* and I felt privileged. I could not imagine not being with Carol and I thought she must feel the same way about me. Sam and Evie thought we were cute and didn't mind that I tied up their telephone for hours at a time talking to my new love. I wanted to shout out to the whole world 'I have a girlfriend!' I wanted to walk down the street hand in hand with Carol and kiss her wherever and whenever I felt the need. I bought her flowers and chocolates, I praised her many wonderful qualities. I wanted to live for my new love. I had no idea how her mind worked though, and thought that if I gave her enough things she would surely love me forever. I thought love was something you could *get* like a job or a place at university. I was very insensitive to Carol's needs and if I thought something she felt was silly, like when she told me she was shy about holding hands in public, I'd simply dismiss it.

Our affair lasted just over three weeks. In the end she would no longer speak to me and ignored me if she saw me in the street. My love was over as was my entire world. I was angry with Carol and deeply depressed. I went to socialist meetings but was just going through the motions. I was no longer interested in politics and couldn't muster the energy to try to care about some injustice or another.

There were two political films playing at the cinema at this time, *Schindler's List*, about the Holocaust, and *In the Name of the Father*, an Irish production starring Daniel Day Lewis, which was about the wrongful imprisonment of four Irish people accused of a terrorist attack in the 1970s. Party members were handing out leaflets at both of these films promoting a march against the neo-Nazi group National Action who had been holding rallies and trying to recruit new members. I saw both films and thought they were excellent, especially *In the Name of the Father*, which dealt with two themes that I was so fascinated with: terrorism and prison. I went to see that film a second time and, while I was paying for my ticket, met a new comrade who had supposedly just arrived from Sydney. His name was Joe and I knew as soon as I met him that he had a 'past'. We got to talking and I found I had a lot in common with him. When we were watching the film he quietly said to me 'I was a terrorist.' My heart started pumping hard. I had met who I secretly wanted to be. Joe was to become my new best friend, I knew it. I wanted to know what he knew and to be just like him.

I soon spent most of my time with Joe, discussing various criminal acts he had committed. I found out his real name was not Joe, that Joe was a pseudonym. He had been released from prison only a month or so ago after serving six years for shooting and wounding a Nazi. Joe was tough, a real bad boy of the left, and I was enthralled. I asked him all about his experiences in prison and in his previous job as a security guard in Israel. I thought that didn't really go with a socialist philosophy, but by that stage didn't care all that much. He encouraged the side of me that loved aggression and political 'direct action' and I soon became too involved to stop myself from falling into his shadowy world. Joe had no money but I had $4000 saved and happily parted with some of it so he could buy an unregistered gun and illegal mail-order items from America. As much as I knew I was in way too far, I was in a constant state of excitement and felt I was being what I had wanted to be all my life.

Perhaps in a moment of remorse for what I was getting up to, I started telling little snippets of my life with Joe to other Party members who were universally shocked. Joe was a controlling character, though, and much as I knew that what I was doing would lead to more serious consequences than getting arrested on a picket line, I was quite scared of him and thought if I backed out he might just use that newly-purchased gun to shoot me. I'd gone way too far and now there seemed no way out. I was fast realising that Joe was not a terrorist and cared little for political action, he was just a particularly screwed-up criminal who wanted me as his sidekick for various illegal actions. We'd also started having a sort of sexual fling, although without actual sex. He'd bought a pair of handcuffs and two truncheons and we'd take turns handcuffing each other, slapping each other and fooling around. I got quite attached to Joe and was torn between my affection for him and my view of him as a dangerous man who I knew would kill with no hesitation.

Joe was planning an armed robbery and wanted me to be involved. I didn't know what to say, half being thrilled by such a dangerous and illegal plan, half thinking about the consequences for both Joe and I and for the victim should it go wrong. Feeling I'd gone way too far already, I agreed to help Joe in a hold-up. He had all these ideas about how he was not going to get caught and even took a chessboard with him, saying that the victim would tell the police the robber had a chessboard and that would lead them in the wrong direction in their investigation. He'd chosen a hairdressing shop where he'd been before, stating that the boss kept the week's takings in the cash register on a Friday night and there was bound to be several thousand dollars there. I thought robbing somewhere that he'd been before, and going in without a balaclava on his head, was fairly stupid but he seemed to know what he was talking about so I went along with it. In an act worthy of the TV show *World's Dumbest Criminals*, Joe got a haircut before pulling the gun on the hairdresser, then had me open the till and take what money was there. Rather than thousands, there was $80 in the till. We stole the poor woman's car and left her tied up in the shop. For the first time in my life I felt guilt and knew I had done something truly awful, something that could not be taken back. I wanted to be caught, thinking that being punished would help me feel better. We got back to Joe's friend's house in the mountains and Joe bought lots of beers and started to drink them. I didn't feel like drinking at all and just sipped at my beer. After about his eighth beer, Joe said he'd drive me home. Given the state Joe was in I knew that getting into a car with him may well be the last thing I ever did, but I resignedly agreed and we got in our stolen car.

Joe drove around every suburb of Melbourne, ignoring my pleas for him to drop me off in Richmond where I lived. We stopped at a petrol station as the car was on empty and I handed him the handbag we'd stolen from the hairdresser, knowing the key to the petrol cap was in there. Joe snatched it off me, saying 'Don't look in there!' (Later I realised Joe had lied about the amount he'd found and that the $2000 that was the hairdresser's takings was in the bag, but at the time I thought nothing of it.) When we were about five minutes' drive away from my house, Joe ran a red light and a police car started chasing us. Joe was drunk and a terrible driver anyway. He crashed the car into a power pole. He told me to 'Go, GO!!' and I jumped out of the car and ran. A huge policeman chased after me and knocked me to the ground and Joe skulked off while the police were spending all their energy on me.

Soon it seemed every police car in Melbourne had showed up in that quiet street and a crowd of people had come out of their houses to watch the drama. Not caring about the large number of witnesses, the large cop who had grabbed me started pushing me around and threatening me, only stopping when he worked out I was a girl. I had my head shaved, was wearing men's clothes and I was very thin, so it was understandable that the policeman thought me male. He then called over a female officer to interrogate me as to my accomplice's whereabouts. She was twice as brutal as her male counterpart, but they eventually believed my story that I had no idea where Joe was. The media had turned up and I soon had to avoid a camera crew as I was being taken to a waiting police car by a couple of uniformed officers.

I was taken to police headquarters in the city centre, this time in very different circumstances from the last time I had been there. I figured that this time I wouldn't be going home with a form to look at for the coming weeks. I thought as I was led through the door, handcuffed, that this would have to be the worst day of my life. A big detective and his smaller colleague played a successful game of 'good cop, bad cop' with me, me being terrified I was about to be beaten and possibly killed if I did not give them the information they wanted. I did not tell them Joe's name or his whereabouts but described my involvement in the previous night's events in great detail. While I was worrying about what the scary detective and his seemingly nicer friend were going to do to me if I didn't tell them Joe's name, they informed me they had caught him anyway, thus saving me from any violence. He had returned to where I had been arrested for some reason and the waiting police officers picked him up without too much trouble. I was somewhat relieved and wanted to speak to Joe, being annoyed that the police would not let me see him. It was 5 am by this stage, but I was offered the chance to phone someone and tried my parents, who were of course still in bed and didn't answer their phone. Not wanting to leave a message on their answering machine saying I had just been arrested for armed robbery, I hung up, hoping I would get to speak to them soon. The detectives then let me phone my housemates but they were out. A few hours later I was driven to my house in Richmond and the police searched my room for evidence. My housemate Evie was there, and was very scared and concerned. I remember asking the detectives if I could say goodbye to my cat, Sensei, and being told no.

I was refused bail at court and remanded to Fairlea Prison. I had never been so scared in all my life, thinking I was going to be beaten up, raped or murdered by my fellow prisoners. I had never known any women ex-prisoners and knew only what I had seen from films and television. A young police officer took me down some stairs to the city watch-house and I had my first experience of women prisoners, meeting Laurie and Emmy. When I was brought in, Laurie, a tough but kind-looking woman with short, dark hair, asked the policeman if they'd made a mistake and said that 'These are the women's cells, mate.' She thought I was a young boy, but when I explained that I was a girl she smiled and introduced herself. She seemed a bit of a hippie and I thought she too might be gay. We got along from the moment we met and I thought that it couldn't be all that scary in prison if there were women like Laurie in there. The other girl, Emmy, was a little older than me and seemed to be trying to be as tough as she could without really succeeding. She had graffitied the cell with toothpaste and didn't seem to have much to say to me. Both women were withdrawing from heroin and I had my first glimpse of that terrible experience, thinking how awful it must be to come off the drug.

The cell was cold and damp, with concrete benches to sit on and nothing to do except watch a TV that the police had turned to the foreign-language channel and wouldn't change to any other station. Meals were brought in three times daily but I gave up on mine after finding mouldy bread in the lunch. We were told the meals were the same as hospital food but I found that hard to believe, thinking patients in a hospital would surely complain if given the tasteless gloop we were being fed. At night we were locked in a cell with foam squares for mattresses and three thin blankets. Laurie showed me how to tie a blanket around three of the squares to make a bed and use the other two blankets to sleep under. It was bitterly cold and uncomfortable but I did finally get off to sleep and had a dream that I was flying through the sky above my parents' farm, navigating mountains and clouds and feeling euphoric and amazed at the beauty of the world. At 8.30 am a policeman came in and yelled 'Purkis!' at me and I was transported from my magical dream into reality. It was a cold shock. Apparently I had a phone call from my parents and this was a great privilege that I should be thankful for. When I got to the phone I was met with my worried and angry mother half-screaming, half-crying at me. She had read a report about my arrest in the newspaper and I thought that maybe I should have left a message on her answering machine, after all. She asked me why I had done what I did and I honestly could not tell her. This worried me immensely and I felt a double surge of the guilt and fear that had been with me the last couple of days. I felt I had descended into a hell of my own making and there was no escape. My mother's reaction only made it more real. I was taken back to my cell through the police officers' recreation room, past happy cops playing pool and laughing, drinking coffee and inhabiting a completely different world from me. I was surprised that anyone could be enjoying themselves and hated the police officers for what I thought was their easy life.

My Irish socialist friend Steven had sent in a packet of smokes for me, even though I hadn't smoked cigarettes since I was about 17. I figured these were for the purpose of sharing with my fellow prisoners so I could make friends. Laurie and Emmy enjoyed the cigarettes and I thought I should probably take up smoking myself so that I could give cigarettes to other women at Fairlea Prison and get on their good sides should they take an instant dislike to me. When my packet of smokes ran out, we searched the floor of the cell for 'bumpers' – butt-ends of our previously smoked cigarettes. I left the bumpers for Emmy and Laurie, thinking their need was greater than mine. I got used to the routine of the watch-house and began to study for my next role – the prisoner. Laurie used words I'd never heard before, jail-slang, and, as I had studied the Australian dialect so many years before, I now studied this strange language. I worked out the main things that upset criminals: hurting children, informing on someone and associating with those that did such things. I thought if I could just follow these rules I would fit in to my new position in the world without too much trouble.

I hoped Fairlea Women's Prison was not as uncomfortable and cold as the cells in the city watch-house but Laurie assured me it was much nicer there and women got to live in units with eight or nine cells in them. I had a picture of Fairlea in my mind that I thought about constantly, but I knew it was bound to be far removed from the actuality of the place. The van that would take us to Fairlea arrived and I was marched past the front desk of the watch-house, past the fat, scary-looking sergeant who looked at me and asked 'What are you in for? Molesting little boys? Or is it little girls?' I did not find this as offensive as most would, but still thought it was pretty rude of him to say such things. He pointed at his video monitor and informed me, in spiteful tones, 'Your boyfriend has just hanged himself. What are you going to do now you're all alone?' Horrified, I craned over his desk to get a better look at the video screen. He laughed and said 'Oh no, wait, he's still breathing.' I glared at him as I was led down the corridor to the waiting prison van.

As I travelled through the streets of Melbourne for the first time as a prisoner I was struck by how hidden the world I had just entered was. I doubted that anyone was aware of the three female prisoners in the back of the police van, so I waved at the cars following us. A truck driver honked his horn and I figured it was probably for me, this cheering me up no end. I wanted the world to know there were those of us who did not follow the rules and who existed in an almost parallel world to them. Without knowing it, I had started to identify with the criminals of the world, rather than my previous fascination, as a socialist, with the workers of the world.

When we finally got to Fairlea Prison, which was situated in an inner suburb of Melbourne near a golf course, we were 'processed', officers taking our details, medical staff questioning us in detail to determine if we had any psychological problems or were a suicide risk. We then went to the clothing store, taken in individually and strip-searched, then given second-hand prison-issue clothes: a blue tracksuit and white t-shirt that had our prisoner number stamped where the label would normally be. I was 102604, a number I memorised instantly. After what seemed an age we were taken to the new-arrivals unit, known as Yarrabrae, carrying two heavy green duffel bags with our prison issue clothes and generic-brand toiletries. It was night time and I couldn't see much of the prison, so I was left still wondering what my new home looked like even after I had arrived.

Emmy and I were sent to one unit, Laurie to another. I thought I would miss Laurie's company, and hoped the other residents of my unit would be friendly and that I would make a good impression. There were three other women in my unit, two 25-year-olds and an older woman, Karen. Karen was a sort of godmother figure who pretty much ran the unit and, while she seemed nice enough, I could tell that crossing her would not be a good idea. Our unit had a lounge-type area with a couch and TV, and had five cells coming off the lounge, four of them with one bunk in, the fifth with two. Hoping I wouldn't have to share with anyone, I was relieved to find that mine had only one bunk. After watching Karen's favourite, the late-night horror movie, I went to my cell and emptied my duffel bag, folding my clothes and stacking them neatly against the wall, there being little cupboard space. I found a thick booklet explaining all the rules of the jail and leafed through it, realising there was not a lot one could do that did not incur a penalty and finding the first page particularly amusing as it said 'Welcome to Her Majesty's Prison Fairlea'. I giggled at my towels, which had 'Property of the Victorian Government' written on them. I thought things must be bad if the government owned my towels. I wanted to do some drawing but for some reason was unable to do so and felt I may never make art again.

The next morning I was woken by a prison officer, a 'screw', unlocking the unit and calling me by my surname, 'Purkis! Get up! Muster.' It was 6.30 am and I wanted to go back to sleep, but thinking I'd better do what I was told, I stumbled out of bed and dragged my blue tracksuit on. Karen told me we all had to stand outside on the 'muster line' and be counted and that this happened three times a day. Leaving the unit at 6.55 I got my first look at Fairlea. It looked like it had been built in the 1970s and I was struck by the lack of bright colours: everything was grey or brown. The place looked depressing and drab and I wanted to paint the walls of the unit purple or orange, just to cheer the place up a bit. After we had been counted we had to go to work. There were several jobs in the prison: industries, which was repetitive process work; gardening, for those who liked the outdoors; billets, who were the cleaners of the units and a good job as you were pretty much your own boss; and the kitchen, which was the prestige job at Fairlea. All the toughest girls worked in the kitchen and the pay was a whopping $6.50 per day, the best in the jail. New inmates usually went to industries as it was the lowest paid job at $4.50 per day. Nervously, wondering what my workmates would be like, I followed the line to industries.

I had worked out that I had to fit in or life was going to be very difficult for me. Surprisingly I found it very easy to play the role of a criminal. There was a strict set of rules that were very easy to learn and prisoners had no problem accepting someone who was a bit different if they followed the rules. Had I been my different self and not worked out what was expected of me, I imagine my life would have been hellish, but I'd had plenty of practice at doing what was expected of me and playing various roles and I had little trouble becoming Jeanette the criminal. I soon had more friends than I'd ever had before, although I was in a constant state of alert, knowing that most of my friends would think nothing of attacking me physically should I do something wrong. I became known as a weird but 'staunch' girl, particularly after a fight I started with the sole intention of being accepted. A new girl had come into our unit, Beth. She was a big girl and was the only person in the prison younger than me: she was 19 and I was 20. After a girl I knew had been in a fight, with no witnesses other than Beth and one other girl, Beth had gone to tell the officers. That night she came back to our unit, all of us knowing she'd told, yet everyone else being too old to hurt such a 'baby'. I picked a fight with her, which ended with her yelling so loudly that the officers came running and unlocked the door, to find me punching her. Just as I thought the authorities in my life were going to make things even more difficult than they already were, Beth grabbed a knife and stabbed me in the head, the result being a trip to the medical centre for me and a trip to the Management Unit, where problem prisoners were kept, for her. I had earned more 'cred' than I could have hoped for. Everyone thought that, even though I had a university education and came from a decidedly middle-class background, I was a decent sort, a 'toff'.

For the first few weeks I was in prison I was obsessed with the wall. I would look at it and longingly think of drinking nice coffee, watching movies at the cinema, my studio space at RMIT, smoking dope and all the other good things I associated with being free. I imagined escaping, and had dreams in which I was told I could leave for a week, as long as I came back. I spent most of my time dwelling on the fact that I was not free. After the first few weeks I forgot where I was and concentrated on my life as a prisoner. I no longer cared what free people could do and I couldn't. Rather, I became totally resigned to where I was and concentrated on doing what I could get away with at Fairlea. I now focused on the things *inside* the wall, rather than those going on on the other side of it. There was no wall to me. The prison had become my world.

My only reminder of the outside world was the letters and visits I received from my parents and friends. I was allowed a total of ten visitors and had to put in a form deciding which ten people I knew who could visit me. When I actually had visits I was torn between the new version of myself and my old personality and never knew exactly what to say to my visitors. My original world was, of course, the world I had known as a student and as a protester. Yet those identities conflicted with my new life as a criminal. I would be embarrassed when my socialist friends visited me, especially Mark, an older man who had been involved in left-wing politics for most of his life. He would loudly discuss the campaign against Jeff Kennett or some other political thing and I would want to disappear into the nearest hole in the ground. Likewise, visits from my friends from RMIT always filled me with a sense of dread as not all of my criminal mates knew I had been to art school and I wasn't about to let them in on what I saw as my guilty secret. My parents and Dean also embarrassed me, and I wished they were a bit rougher, like everyone else's families seemed to be. I wished I at least had a stepfather or some family problems, rather than my actual parents who had only had one fight in my life-time as far as I knew.

While my parents embarrassed me for their lack of street-cred they were a useful source of funds. I had no problem with ringing them and asking for money whenever I was short of cigarettes or wanted a special treat like a chocolate bar to have with my dinner. I would ring them on one of the three pay phones in the jail and plead for $30 or $50, making up some excuse as to why I had no money. They always obliged and I was able to help my friends out when they ran out of cigarettes or had a fine from the prison's internal court. I was even more popular because I always had a smoke for anyone who needed one, and never went without myself. I had seen women who everyone took cigarettes off and never paid back, but in my mind I was not one of these apparently weak characters, I was just generous.

I still had my obsession with authority to contend with, and the fact that I actually was in the belly of the beast, so to speak, did not keep me satisfied for long. While far from a model prisoner, I stayed out of trouble for the first couple of months in Fairlea but I soon grew tired of being 'good' and thought I should stir things up a bit to make life more interesting. At first, I thought the screws were simply items of human furniture who owned a useful set of keys that let me out in the morning and, while I didn't particularly like many of them, I wasn't too bothered by them. Some of them seemed to spend most of their time trying to do some good for the women prisoners and to try to make their lives easier, but quite a few seemed to have taken a position with the Office of Corrections to be a figure of power and authority and to use their power to make prisoners' lives hard. While these officers were in the minority, their presence was certainly felt by all and I started to feel the need to let them know I had no intention of being bossed about.

As I had when attending violent political protests, I began to revel in confronting screws who I thought had overstepped the mark. My first target was Mr Darville, one of the officers who supervised industries. He was my boss at work and would not give his employees a cigarette break. He reported anyone who snuck off to the toilets for a cigarette to the governor. He was rude to the women and would make cracks about them being 'fat' or 'ugly' and delighted in telling us all what slow workers we were and how we would never find work outside of prison. One day Mr Darville made a rude comment to me and told me to 'Get on with it Purkis, we're not on the picket line now' and without thinking I told him to 'Get fucked!' He sacked me and marched me, handcuffed, through the prison to Yarrabrae where women who had been put on loss of privileges (solitary confinement and no cigarettes) were held. Thinking I was to be locked up in solitary, or 'the slot' as it was known, I verbally abused him with every insult I could think of. He then threw me into a yard and locked it behind me. I'd heard of this place but never seen it; it was 'the cage' where women who had been sacked from their jobs were kept. Mr Darville also informed me he was writing me up and I would have to face the prison governor in the prison's internal court. I insulted Mr Darville some more and found a spot in the shade, sitting there for another three hours until the work day was finished. I spent two weeks in the cage during work hours, most of it by myself with nothing to do except pace and think. I was paid nothing for the two weeks I was unemployed, having to rely on other prisoners and my parents to pay for coffee and cigarettes. I also had to move from my cell in one of the 'cottage' units to a less pleasant cell in Yarrabrae.

As I had been addicted to militant protests before being imprisoned, I was now addicted to flouting authority and making a nuisance of myself in jail. I swam naked in the prison's small swimming pool and was written up for that. I flashed my bum at a screw, saying 'This one's for you!' to the officer, and was written up for that. I smuggled cigarettes to the girls in solitary and got caught for that and written up. I was gathering a large number of prison charges and had several governor's hearings pending, but I didn't really care as I was satisfying my wish to be a 'bad girl' and on the wrong side of the considerably powerful authority of the prison officers.

I had moved back into my old cell in cottage two and had found work in another part of industries – this time snipping threads off green sheets and folding them to be shipped off to wherever they went to be sold. My new cellmate was a 40-year-old woman called Liz who was one of the many older women who doted on me and called me 'the baby'. Liz had a little business organised whereby she would get her boyfriend to throw a tennis ball full of drugs over the wall and sell them to the other women in the unit for cigarettes. About two days after I moved in with her, the officers searched our cell and found a large number of the paints and plaster figurines made at my old job in industries in a drawer on my side of the cell (I think the person who had lived in the cell before me had put them there). The other women told me Liz would want to kill me, as she would have governor's court and be denied visits and would therefore be unable to tell her boy-friend when to drop the drugs off. I had to front up to her and let her know what had happened. I was very scared and thought I was in for the beating of my life. When I told her she grunted, looked like she wanted to hurt me and then said, 'Well, that's done then. If you do it again you'll be sorry.' Relieved, I went back to my unit, thanking whatever higher power there was in the universe that I had not had the crap beaten out of me.

Liz's drugs kept most of the unit happy on Saturday nights and I felt a little left out, hearing the party as I went to sleep but never being asked to join in. I worked out that the other women didn't want to give me drugs because they thought I hadn't tried them before, so I told Laurie, who was living in our unit at this time, a lie that I'd tried speed (amphetamines) at parties before and enjoyed the experience. She passed this on to Liz and the next time the drugs came in I was offered a 'taste'. Delighted, I drank the foul-tasting mixture of speed and water and waited for something to happen. I spent the next few weekends speeding and euphoric, usually making use of the high to clean the unit, vacuuming and dusting as if my life depended on it. One time some of the women had taken other drugs, valium and the like, mixed with their speed and were quite aggressive as the two substances should not really be mixed. Liz was in a foul mood and tried to take it out on me, not that I really cared, thinking she was not in her right mind. My friend and new cellmate, Kathy, stood up for me, putting Liz in her place, and then proceeded to give me a hard time, telling me to 'Fight your own battles!' The next day I pretended I had been sleeping all night as the officers came in to wake us up for the morning head-count. I knew our unit had been making noise all night and that the screws would suspect we were on drugs, so I did my best to pretend I had not been using anything other than the sleeping pills I was prescribed by the medical centre. The next day my entire unit was taken to be tested for drugs. We were strip-searched and had to urinate in front of a female prison officer – the urine being sent off for drug-testing. I knew what the result would be and what the punishment for drug use was – seven days in solitary and loss of visits. Sure enough, we all tested positive and had to go to governor's court. Karen assured us, every time we took drugs, that drinking a cup of pure vinegar would cleanse our systems of anything prohibited, and had insisted we all drink the foul stuff every time we had a 'party'. This apparently was false. We all spent a week in 'the slot' and had to wear a visit suit with 'Identified Drug User' printed on the back of it when our visits were reinstated. This suit zipped up at the back and came with a plastic tag that made it impossible for anyone to slip anything into it during visits, not that that worried me. I was more concerned by the fact that my parents would know I had been taking drugs and made up elaborate lies that I had been smoking joints, thinking marijuana a lesser evil than speed in the eyes of my mum and dad.

Prisoners were allowed four sessions of education a week and could go during work hours. I put off going for a long time, thinking the classes would probably be basic and boring but, on advice from Laurie and others, I finally decided to see what the Education Centre had to offer. The teachers were so unlike the officers that I couldn't believe they worked in the same environment. They were all women and seemed genuinely interested in the lives of the prisoners. There were many classes we could take, ranging from maths to English to the ones I liked, such as drama, art and creative writing. I liked the drama teachers, Maud and Kharen, instantly. They had started a drama group for women prisoners and ex-prisoners called 'Somebody's Daughter Theatre Company' in the early 1980s. They were the most caring people I had come across at Fairlea and did whatever they could to make the prisoners' lives easier. I had never heard of this theatre company before but soon found out they had been awarded a number of arts grants and had quite a reputation on the outside world. I loved going to drama class and wished I could be paid full-time for drama rather than being bored at work in industries. In drama class we would laugh about one thing or another and generally have lots of fun. Maud and Kharen had planned a new production and we were given the job of writing the script and the songs, even coming up with most of the ideas for the play (which was called *The Cosmic Laundromat* and dealt with the idea of women finding their true self and their soul after a life of hardship). I lived for the four hours each week that I spent at the education centre, writing song lyrics and thinking up ideas for the play with the other women, or having my horoscope drawn up by Maud and Kharen's American astrologer friend.

I had started drawing again and had attracted the attention of the toughest girl in the prison while sketching my self-portrait one day. Katrina was serving a minimum of 15 years for a double murder committed when she was 20. She had a short fuse and everyone stepped carefully when she was around. Katrina was in the education centre when I was doing one of the best self-portraits I had ever done. She remarked on how good my drawing was and asked me to draw a portrait of her cellmate, Melanie. This suggestion filled me with utter terror; I may have been an expert at self-portraits, but had never managed to draw anyone else successfully. I knew that if I refused my life would become fairly unpleasant, so I accepted Katrina's offer of payment (a packet of Peter Jackson cigarettes) and went over to her cottage, pencil in hand, wondering what would happen to me when I inevitably made a terrible drawing of Melanie. I concentrated on the drawing as I never had before but it was still a pitiful attempt. Luckily Melanie didn't mind, so Katrina thought it was funny rather than insulting and I was saved. I left the cottage after a cup of coffee and some leftover lunch and was invited back in again should I ever want to visit.

My court case was approaching, causing me less nervousness than maybe it should. I was used to prison and, for the first time in my life, was liked by almost everyone I knew. I liked the routine of prison life and the fact that there was usually someone to talk to. I knew I was looking at some more time, maybe another two years or so, but rather than worrying me, this fact actually cheered me up no end. I would read the brief of evidence against me provided by the police and actually enjoy the experience, almost feeling proud to be such a 'bad girl'. My family and friends from RMIT all wanted me to be released but I thought another two years as a prisoner would be great and would prove to everyone what a serious, tough criminal I was.

My solicitor, Vince, had started visiting me regularly and had advised me to plead guilty due to my confession to the police and the large amount of other evidence against me. I thought this an easier course of action than a trial, which would last probably a couple of weeks and would mean I had to spend the time I wasn't in the court room in the watch-house, not a nice place. Vince was trying to find something that would mean I got less time than it looked like I was going to and, wanting to seem like I was taking an active interest in proceedings, I went along with this. My mum had been speaking with a workmate who had a son that my mum thought sounded just like me. My parents had thought me strange my whole life, but had never known why, and even the psychiatrists I had been sent to had been puzzled by my apparently inexplicable behaviour. My mum's work friend said her son had been diagnosed with something called Asperger Syndrome, which was related to autism, something my parents had never heard of but which sounded very much like what had made me so different. There were only two professionals in Melbourne at that time who could diagnose it and my parents contacted the psychologist who worked with adults with Asperger Syndrome, Vicki Batista. She agreed to come to the prison and conduct the relevant tests.

When I heard my parents speak of the possibility that I had this condition I was torn between wanting to know why I was strange and feeling that my parents were just trying to feel better about themselves by finding an explanation for my bad behaviour. I did the tests Vicki gave me and found some of the tasks incredibly easy, especially the ones in which I had to memorise series of numbers. The test in which I had to arrange a set of cards with cartoons of social situations in order totally threw me and I ended up just guessing, hoping I'd put them in the correct order but having no idea of what went where. Vicki asked me many questions about my childhood and my reasons for my actions. A short while later my parents told me she had diagnosed me with Asperger Syndrome and that it was the reason I felt no remorse for bad behaviour and didn't have any ability to empathise with people, including the victim of my crime. It was also why I could not recognise people's faces or facial expressions and why I found body language and non-verbal communication so hard to fathom. All of a sudden I had a reason for all the problems that had made my life so difficult and had left me wondering how other people 'work' and why I had trouble keeping friends. I was torn between a sense of relief and a stronger feeling, the knowledge that I was fundamentally different from most people and that there was nothing I could do to be like others. I had been running from my difference all my life and trying to be like other people, something I now knew was impossible. Deep down I knew what Vicki had said was true and that I did have this thing everyone was telling me I did, but on the surface I wanted to be the same, to be included. I refused to accept that I had Asperger Syndrome and went back to my 'normal' act. I was a good actress and even convinced myself that I was like other people. I didn't listen to my parents when they told me the new things they discovered all the time about Asperger Syndrome.

The diagnosis was a huge advantage for my court case and my lawyer told me I might only have to spend a few more months in Fairlea or that I may even be released at court. I had mixed emotions about this and sometimes hoped I would get out, but sometimes wished for a longer sentence. The drama teachers' astrologer friend had told me I would get what I expected at court and I expected to get out. I didn't know whether to be happy about this or not. When I got to court I was excited. I'd been to court before but only for protesting, nothing as serious as this time. I felt that my life was in the hands of the judge, a thought that scared me and thrilled me all at once. It was the first time I had seen my co-accused, Joe, since that night six months ago when I had left him in our stolen car in Richmond. I spent a fair while whispering insults to Joe, so much so that my lawyer came over and advised me it was not helping my case any. My step-grandmother Pauline had come to court, as had my parents and some friends from RMIT. I was very nervous and didn't want my friends and family to hear all the bad things I'd done six months ago. The judge heard the evidence from the prosecutor and Joe's and my barristers. He said we had to come back the next day to be sentenced. I spent a nervous night in solitary, having been sent there for another positive drug test, hardly sleeping and wishing I had someone to talk to or at least some cigarettes to calm my nerves. When I returned to court, the judge sentenced Joe to two years and six months and me to the six months I'd already served with an 18-month suspended sentence. I was a free woman unless I committed any crimes in the next 18 months. I was taken to the cells to be signed out, worrying for a while as the governor of Fairlea had said I needed to serve the rest of my time in solitary, another four days. Thankfully the court seemed to have more influence in the matter than the prison governor and I collected my jacket and walked out the door to where my family were waiting.

6.

Losing Friends and Gaining Contacts

My friends from RMIT, Sharon and Lee, had told the court I could stay with them until I found somewhere more permanent so I moved into their house in the inner suburb of North Melbourne. They lived above a shop in a fantastic, artily-decorated flat full of trinkets, paintings and beautiful rugs Sharon's dad had supplied. I was given use of the spare bedroom and slept on a mat on the floor. As I could sleep almost anywhere and in any position I had no problem with this, although I wished the room didn't feel so much like a storage cupboard. Lee and Sharon were both still studying and had jobs, so I spent most of my time alone in their house.

I had a lot of trouble adjusting to life as a free person. I would wake up at 6 am expecting to have to stand on the muster line and be counted before breakfast. I kept wondering what to do and why my day was so unstructured, thinking a day's work at industries would be a pleasant change to sitting around the house waiting for my friends to come home. I missed my criminal pals and wrote them all long letters most days. When I returned to Fairlea by taxi to collect my belongings,

I had a long conversation with the officer on duty at the gate and wondered if they might let me in on weekends. I rang all the people I had known before being imprisoned and found, to my surprise, that most of them wanted nothing to do with me. I was particularly upset when my artist friends, George and Julie, told me they never wanted to see me again. I sat at the kitchen table and wept, wondering why nobody wanted my company. I didn't think I was a bad person and couldn't see why others would.

About two days after my release I went to the bank to withdraw some of the $3500 I thought was in my account. I had lent my bank card to my old housemate, Evie, while still in prison as I owed her money for rent. I was unaware that she and her boyfriend, Sam, were both heroin addicts and the fact that they had withdrawn my entire savings came as a complete surprise. The bank would not refund the money and I was left with nothing. I found Evie and Sam's phone number after trying to track them down for weeks and, when I called them, they claimed the theft was 'compensation' for my bringing the police to their house.

I was being paid unemployment benefits and I started spending most of my fortnightly cheque on marijuana, finding I only felt good if I was stoned. I would go to parties, not to meet people but to see if there was any free dope going around. I made everyone at one party laugh by addressing them in criminal slang. They were unable to decipher what I said and I had to translate. I smoked most days and looked forward to buying a new deal more than anything else. I spent a lot of time in the company of two women who'd been in prison with me, Frankie and Kiera. They both had children and ex-husbands to worry about, but they weren't too bothered about either, preferring to drink beer or smoke drugs and forget their problems. I would travel to their houses in the outer suburbs, getting on the train without a ticket and drinking beer most of the way, to go to score drugs with them. They both used amphetamines and I started 'doing speed' with them, enjoying the invincible feeling that drug gave me. One day Frankie and Kiera came to Sharon and Lee's house and left the syringes they'd injected the speed with in the bin. I was scared of the consequences should Lee or Sharon find the needles and went to great lengths to hide them, wrapping them in tissues and pushing them inside a milk carton before throwing them back into the bin.

After I had lived with Lee and Sharon for a month or so things got difficult and I found myself the subject of many a discussion. They were worried about my continual drug use and concerned that, should I be caught, my suspended sentence would come into effect and I would end up at Fairlea once more. I thought they were worrying about nothing and refused to listen, saying that I knew what I was doing and 'Don't worry!' Eventually Lee told me I would have to find somewhere else to live. The outside world didn't seem as great as people seemed to think it was. I thought my life in prison was much more fun than life outside, where people betrayed me and stole from me and expected what seemed totally unreasonable things from me.

I set about looking for a house and discovered that nobody wanted a housemate who was stoned, unkempt and had just been released from prison. I went to what felt like hundreds of share-house interviews, all with the same outcome – they didn't want me. At one house I was even told by some sympathetic and well-intentioned Catholic students that they'd found someone who needed the house more than me as he was homeless. I thought I would be homeless if I didn't find somewhere soon but it looked like I had no hope of finding accommodation. I was unemployed and had little prospect of finding work, and I also felt there was no shame in my having been in prison and had a habit of telling my prospective housemates where I'd been for the past six months. I finally found a room in a boarding house not far from Sharon and Lee's house. The rent was far more than I wanted to pay but I was out of options. I borrowed money for the security deposit from my parents and moved into my new home, hoping I'd have something in common with the other occupants of the house, the people I had to share the kitchen and bathroom with.

Before long I was missing the company of Sharon and Lee and feeling very lonely in my big, empty room. I had no structure to my days and could never think of how to fill in time. I did some drawing and some painting, watched a video and listened to music, but that still left a lot of time with nothing to do. My room had no aerial connection for my TV so I could only watch videos and I could only afford to rent five videos a week. I would watch my films over and over. This was a practice that had always given me great pleasure in the past, as I could work out the characters' motivations and intentions on about the fourth or fifth viewing of a film and by the eighth or ninth time I knew what their facial expressions meant. Knowing what the next line in the film was had always been comforting, too. However, the films I watched now were violent, negative, disturbing and depressing ones; I could not bring myself to watch anything happy. These films only ever increased my somewhat desperate mood. Dark movies had always made me feel good as they were a link to the dark worlds of my fantasy, but now my world had actually become a dark one and I was finding it a lot less satisfying than I had imagined.

My fellow boarders were all men and most of them had social problems. The man in the room next to me was an English immigrant who had overstayed his visa. He was often drunk and always scary, frequently telling me how he thought the Irish 'should be exterminated. Are there any good Irish people? NO!' and making the sign of a gun pointing to his head every time he mentioned a girl he was obsessed with. I was terrified of this man and thought him more than capable of murder as well as being a frightful right-wing bigot. I even wrote a poem about him, which ended 'While I sold grass in my room, you sold your soul in yours.' One day he knocked on my door and urgently told me of his plans to flee the country as the immigration department were looking for him. He left me detailed instructions about what to do with his belongings should they deport him.

The man on the other side of me was a young drug addict who spent most of his time at rave parties taking LSD and ecstasy. He came across as unfathomable and I often wondered what he had done in his past that he wasn't letting on about. He taped some of his techno music for me and would share his drugs sometimes. We'd discuss the kinds of things that drug addicts do and listen to the music, thinking we were enjoying it all the more for the illegal substances we'd just taken. He had a turquoise ring that he loved and one day I found it near the sink in the kitchen. Without a thought I pocketed it, lying to the best of my ability to him when he asked if I had seen it. I gave it to my criminal friend, Kiera, and spent the rest of the time I lived in that house worrying that she would bump into him while wearing it and I would get into trouble.

My only company most of the time was my cat, Sensei, who seemed to me to be taking on whatever emotional state I was in at any given time. She would stare out the window for hours if I was depressed or jump around and play should I be in a happy mood. I'd always been close to my cat but now I saw her as a true friend and someone that I could rely on. I had few human friends at the time, although I did spend some time with my old housemate's ex-girl-friend, Jane, who lived a few streets away. I'd go to her place and try to ignore her lack of personal hygiene and the usual smattering of used condoms lying on the floor. She had visited me in prison a few times and written me many chatty letters, complete with poems and drawings. I cooked her many a vegetarian curry at my house and we'd talk for hours about anything and everything.

One day Jane took me along to a Socialist Party meeting. I was a bit apprehensive; I'd been expelled from the Party after my arrest, as had my accomplice, Joe. We went to the pub where the meeting was being held and walked into the meeting room late. The leader of the branch looked up as we entered and said 'Only four people have ever been expelled from this organisation. One for rape, one for crossing a picket line and two for armed robbery, and there's one of them now, creeping back into the room.' Feeling unwelcome and embarrassed I left and sat at the bar, drinking beer until the meeting finished and Jane came out. The Party was going through major factional issues and my entering the room had been an excuse for the leader to have a go at oppositional members of the Party. A few weeks later Jane told me she was going to England, but that she'd write often. She never wrote and I heard two years later that she was homeless and begging for change in London, donating half of what she was given to environmental charities.

I started to spend a lot of time in the company of Kiera and Frankie, my friends from Fairlea. They were now going out with each other and would either be loving and sweet to each other or would fight. We would go to a pub and every time we were there Kiera would start a fight and we would be thrown out. One day Frankie wanted to drive home after drinking 12 or so beers and Kiera threw her keys on top of a building to prevent her from doing so. We hitched home and Frankie went back the next day to get her keys, cursing her girlfriend. I felt at home with Kiera and Frankie. Being with them was like being back at Fairlea and deep down that's where I wanted to be. I didn't mind travelling for two hours to get to their house, or having to put up with their frequent fights. Frankie's youngest daughter, Jemma, would cheer me up by pronouncing my name wrong, calling me 'Jex'. We'd drive through the night, on a mission to buy drugs, usually. We would buy speed most weeks and stay up all night chatting, drinking and playing up.

Frankie lived in her mum's house and there was no spare room for me so I'd sleep on the floor, having to listen to Kiera and Frankie having sex in the bed next to me. I didn't mind and was never embarrassed by their intimacy, but I always felt a bit left out. One night, just after Frankie had moved into her new Housing Commission house, she and I had a dope-smoking competition, which lasted most of the night. We matched each other, bong for bong, until, after each of us had smoked about 40 bongs in a row, Frankie gave up and I was declared the champion smoker. I was so proud I didn't even mind that the drugs had been paid for entirely by me and basically we'd smoked a week's supply in one night. Another night the child welfare worker came around to make sure Frankie was being a responsible mother. We had to be on our best behaviour. I had smoked too many bongs and drunk some beers, so when the welfare worker came around she took one look at me and asked 'What's she on? Heroin?'

I was smoking marijuana pretty much all day every day, not eating well and only just managing to pay the rent. A friend of a friend who worked in an ice-cream shop down the street where I lived would tell me every time I was in her shop that I smoked too much, remarking each time I came in 'Are you stoned *again*?' I was doing some work for universities as a nude model for drawing classes and the extra money was a huge bonus, meaning I could buy drugs most days and still pay the rent. Retaining something of my impressive work ethic, I would never go to work stoned and was always on time for jobs, but I lost some work as teachers from the universities often saw me wandering around the inner city stoned as stoned can be. I had a habit of rolling a big joint and smoking it right there in the street and, not caring about any possible legal consequences, I'd pass the joint to anyone I saw who looked like they might be a dope-smoker. I often went to see movies in my drugged state, hardly able to remember the plot after I left the cinema.

On the rare occasions I was not stoned I could usually be found at a drama workshop with Somebody's Daughter Theatre Company, the drama group I had met in prison. They had a rule that none of the participants in their groups could work under the influence of drugs or alcohol so I had a couple of days a week 'straight', going along to drama classes. Maud and Kharen were very supportive and I loved spending time with them and the other actors, all of them women who had been in prison, but most of whom had been released a long time ago. The play I had helped work on in prison was still going ahead; the script was finished and performance dates, both inside and outside the jail, had been arranged for a few months' time. I offered to design and paint the set and this gave me an opportunity to use my creativity and stay off the drugs, at least for the time I was working on the set. I envisioned a set themed on Tibetan mandala patterns, having seen some Tibetan monks making a sand mandala at a city gallery and thinking that would look good and also fit with the spiritual themes of the play. The stage the set was for was a small one so I thought it would be good to cover the floor with a mandala pattern painted on a giant piece of canvas. The job involved a few weeks' painting in the set-design studio at a local theatre. In payment I was given free tickets to various plays and also a session with a psychic who Maud assured me was 'one of the best'. I painted a large perspex backdrop and constructed several fabric covers for the cardboard washing machines that were the main props for the production. I had help with the floor piece in the form of an artist who knew Maud and Kharen, Sandra. She was a little older than me and I was somewhat in awe of her. She liked the work I was doing for Somebody's Daughter Theatre and asked me to help design a set for a performance being put on by some actor friends of hers. I was completely flummoxed by this successful, interesting artist wanting my input on a project and wondered why she did. I still had no confidence in my artistic capabilities and thought I was inferior to most artists. I did a little work for the production, then vanished, giving no thought to the actors needing a set or to Sandra needing another artist.

I enjoyed seeing the free theatrical productions that were my payment for the set design I'd done and wished I could afford to pay to see plays all the time. The theatre was home to a few experimental drama groups and the plays were mostly contemporary and challenging. I was a little worried about the trip to the psychic that had been paid for, though. While I had some faith in such things, four years as a socialist had instilled a large amount of scepticism about all things of a spiritual or paranormal nature and I thought the $80 the session cost could have been better spent on something useful, although at this stage I probably thought something useful equated to drugs. The psychic, Robyn, did not fit my expectations of a clairvoyant and seemed very down-to-earth and sensible and not the flaky, vague, hippieish person I'd imagined. She looked at my palm and looked in the crystal ball, then held the amethyst ring my girlfriend Carol had given me the previous year and finally took out her tarot cards and read them for me. She predicted many things that I could not imagine but got my attention when she said that a 'man sitting in a legal seat' had power over me for another 18 months but that if I avoided trouble for that long his power would disappear. The length of my suspended jail sentence was 18 months and that was also how much longer it was effective for at that time. To my knowledge the clairvoyant did not know anything about me prior to my visit and would therefore have not have known my legal situation. I still found it hard to believe that in the next six months I would be in hospital and that in the next two years I would meet an important partner or that I would lose someone close to me in the next few months. She finally told me of seven symbols that would be important to me for the rest of my life. They included a spider, a cat, a star and a dolphin dancing over the waves. I left feeling a little confused yet still fairly convinced that such things were merely guesswork and superstition.

About six months after my release from prison I had an offer to move into a house in Richmond, a house full of my favourite kind of people at the time: drug dealers. I'd been visiting this house for a couple of months and thought it was wonderful. There was always someone awake at any hour of the day or night and everybody in the house knew where to get hold of whatever substance I happened to want at the time. Two people I knew from my days protesting at the Richmond school picket lived in this house and it was them that were moving out. The idea of moving into a dealer's house, where no one complained if you were stoned and it was always easy to get hold of drugs, appealed to me more than anything. I took no convincing and decided to move in. My friend from Fairlea, Laurie (who had been released before I got out), helped me move and shared a couple of pre-mixed cans of bourbon and coke with me to celebrate my moving into my new home.

When I moved in I paid my first month's rent in advance, but before long I was woefully behind in payments, not that it mattered all that much as all my housemates were also behind in rent. The landlord was the next-door neighbour. He owned the pub that backed onto our house and our feelings of hatred were mutual. We would steal expensive bottles of wine from the bottle shop behind his pub when he wasn't looking and he would threaten us with anything from the police to eviction to physical violence. His heart must have sank every time he saw the ragged bunch of druggies that we were stumbling home early in the morning after a heavy night. He must have known he would never get rent from us and the longer it went on, the more determined we became to live in our house for free. The only bill we paid was the gas bill as it was the coldest winter in years and we couldn't do without our gas heater. The phone and electricity were cut off but we didn't mind; there was a telephone box just down the street and we had batteries for the stereo if we really needed entertaining.

Our reason for existence was to get high and that was pretty much all that we did.

A couple of weeks before moving to my new house I had taken a course for life models that meant I was now on a list of models that every art school had access to – I would be able to work much more often and earn more money. The problem was that the day I moved in the telephone was cut off and none of my potential employers could contact me. I didn't mind, though, as I now had more time to get high and work would have cut into my dope-smoking time. I was living exclusively on government benefits, having to lodge a form every two weeks confirming that I'd looked for work. I had no intention of looking for work, but somehow managed to convince the authorities that I was actively seeking employment. I developed a system for making the small amount of money I was paid last the fortnight. The system involved buying a large quantity of marijuana and making it last two weeks by carefully rationing it. The money I had left over after buying dope went on cat food and, theoretically, on food for me. I always bought food for my cat but the food budget I intended to spend on myself usually ended up going to the drug dealer. If I was feeling overly extravagant on pay day I would buy amphetamines or LSD. I would wake up and start smoking dope, only stopping when I stumbled into bed. I felt I could not stand my own company without drugs and was terrified of being 'straight'. While I thought I'd enjoyed myself in prison and longed to go back, in reality it had left me damaged and unable to cope with life. I didn't listen to the advice of friends who told me I smoked too much dope, thinking them to be echoing the sentiments of my parents.

My twenty-first birthday arrived and I didn't need to think too hard about what I wanted: drugs and lots of them. My parents had given me two gifts, one of them something I knew I would treasure forever, a photo album comprised mainly of pictures of me, as a baby, as a teenager and as an adult. The other gift gave me another excuse to think my parents did not love me, understand me or care for me. The second gift was a street map of Melbourne, a 'Melways'. I had wanted something personal that I could remember the event of my twenty-first by, and the photo album was just that, not that I could see it at the time. Yet, to me, the street directory summed up my feelings towards my mum and dad at the time. I pawned the thing a couple of weeks later and spent the money from it on marijuana, thinking that a fitting end to such a thoughtless present. On the actual day of my birthday I awoke realising I had hardly any money and that I had not organised a party. I spent the day travelling to the houses of all my dope-smoking friends, asking around to see if any of them had any drugs. Late in the evening a girl I'd met twice before came over and offered me a smoke with her. Miserably, I said to her 'It's my twenty-first today.' She replied 'Well, you're celebrating, aren't you?' Two days later I was invited to the house of the art teacher from Fairlea. Laurie was there as well and they had baked a chocolate cake, which the art teacher had decorated with all sorts of wonderful things, including ballerina dolls dressed in skirts made of little sheets of copper and all kinds of sparkly things. They went to the kitchen and came out with a pair of scissors, which I hoped with all my heart were for chopping up a gram of dope. I was disappointed when they told me the scissors were for opening my present. I left, torn between feelings of gratitude to the both of them for throwing me a little party and of anger at the lack of drugs I was given. I lived, breathed and thought dope. It was my reason for being. I was never sober and dreaded having no money with which to buy drugs.

I heard someone say once that drug addicts do not have friends, they only have contacts. That was certainly true of me. I knew so many people but none of them actually could be described as having been my friends; they were just people to hang out with and smoke bongs with. If anything terrible had happened to me they would probably not have done anything to help, nor would they have cared. My housemates and I were close only for as long as there were drugs. We played card games, watched TV and listened to our enormous collection of records and CDs, but we had nothing more in common than our shared interest in getting high. The male members of our household all loved watching the football, but the three women in the house hated the sport and dreaded the weekend; the TV would be on and the house full of the sound of the football commentary. I remarked once to one of the guys that he cared more about his football team than he did about me and I think that may actually have been the case. There were two couples in our house but there didn't seem to be a lot of love. One girl, Penny, went psychotic from speed withdrawal and chased her boyfriend around with a knife, thinking, for some reason, that he was having an affair with me. I was in contact with no one from my past, apart from my family and my criminal friends Kiera and Frankie, who would come over every so often and smoke dope with us. I lost them eventually, too. They had said they would buy my little TV and my VCR for $50 each. I had paid a lot more than that for them, but that was in a previous life, a totally different world to the one I now inhabited. Kiera kept promising to pay me and I trusted her, hoping the $50 would come the next time she visited so that I could buy more drugs. They kept asking me to sell them my stereo, a beautiful machine that I had bought second-hand for $500 when I was working. I flatly refused to sell this as I loved it and had no intention of parting with it, but Kiera and Frankie became increasingly insistent in their demands. One night they came over with some pills. I don't know exactly what they were, some kind of psychiatric medication, perhaps. They gave them to me, along with a cask of white wine. In a few hours I was so drunk I could hardly stand up. They said they were going home and I said goodbye, leaving them to let themselves out. The next day in a state of half-sleep I thought I'd had a dream that my stereo had been stolen and then, when I fully awoke, I realised it actually had. My supposed 'best mates' had helped themselves to my beloved stereo. I never saw or heard from them again.

I was still in contact with my family and went to the pay phone at the bottom of the street to call them reverse charges every Saturday morning. I never missed a Saturday and would try hard to think up something I had been spending my time doing that my parents would approve of. One day I was deep in conversation with my mum about my brother Dean, who I had started to resent and despise, thinking he was 'perfect' while I was a screw-up. I'd come to blame him for all my problems and accuse him of things that I'm sure he would never have done. My mum told me he had a new, 18-year-old girlfriend and I commented that he was 'a sexual pervert'. Just at that moment the phone cut out. I was convinced I'd offended my mother deeply and she had hung up on me. I was too scared to call her back and didn't speak to either of my parents for another six months.

I had started back at RMIT. The university authorities had kindly agreed to take me back even though I'd been in prison only one year ago. I attended an interview with the head of department, managing to offend him by complaining that he kept me waiting for an hour, and was relieved when he said I could come back to finish off second year. I was nervous about being in a new class with new people but was determined to finish my studies, even if it meant not speaking to anyone in my year. Most in my class were quite wary of me as they knew the reason I had deferred my studies the previous year.

I spent most of my time with the people who I'd studied with the year before who were now in their final year. I was too involved in the world of drugs to really care about my studies and soon found myself failing everything. I rarely came to classes and paid little attention in the ones I did attend. I had to write an essay and do a class presentation for art history and I did no research for either, putting them off to the last minute, but knowing they would never get done. I hardly ever went into my studio and when I did I was too scared of the comments from the others in my year to concentrate on anything. My old housemate Jose had become editor of the student newspaper, along with some socialist friends, and I would go to the newspaper office and smoke drugs in the back room. Poor Jose would tell me off, worried about the reaction of campus security should they discover me, but I didn't listen. I took a student loan, which I had no intention of repaying. I eventually withdrew from my course without even finishing second year. I didn't care that I'd failed at something I once cared about. I was too deep in the life of drugs to realise my world was getting more and more difficult as time went on. I was in total denial of all the problems that I was inviting.

I had started taking LSD with some friends of friends I'd met at a party. Initially I loved the effect of this drug and felt like Alice in Wonderland every time I took it. I thought I had a psychic connection with people when on LSD and believed that, for the first time ever, I could actually understand what made people work. I had heard druggies laughingly say that anyone who has taken eight LSD 'trips' is clinically insane. I thought if I was insane it wasn't such a bad way to be; I was having fun. One night my tripping friends and I went to a dance party and 'dropped' our LSD trips. At first I was having a good time, but then a girl from third year at RMIT came up to me and told me she'd just had an abortion and was feeling terrible about it and my night was ruined. I thought everyone in the room was dancing to a pattern and that I was the only person who didn't know what to do. I saw people laughing and knew they were laughing at me for being such a weirdo and for not being able to understand their world. The worst moment was when a cute girl came up to me and told me I was 'a great dancer'. In my drugged state I had no idea that she was probably trying to pick me up. Rather, I thought she was having a joke at my expense and turned on her, snarling 'What do you mean?' and walked off. I could not speak when we got back to my friends' house after the party and so could not communicate how I felt. I eventually calmed down enough to croak out 'I've just had a bad trip' to my friends, who all seemed to be having too much fun to care.

My housing situation had become problematic as we had not paid any rent for three months. The landlord had sent us a solicitor's letter telling us to pay the $900 we owed or get out. I found this letter in the mail box and, as I was very stoned at the time, thought the best thing to do with it would be to throw it in the bin and forget all about it. A couple of weeks later we got an eviction notice, which referred to the previous letter. Everyone was surprised and angrily complained that we hadn't been warned or given a chance to pay the rent. I tried not to look guilty and joined in the accusations against the landlord, thinking I probably shouldn't have thrown the letter out and hoping no one would ever find out what I had done. We had a few weeks to find somewhere else to live and everyone else seemed to have somewhere to go. I couldn't find anywhere to live and was getting more and more stressed as the days went by. My continued use of marijuana, LSD and speed had left me very fragile emotionally and the impending threat of homelessness did nothing to help this. I was too frazzled to actually look at share-houses and knew that nobody would want a skinny, dirty and slightly crazy drug addict moving into their house, anyway.

Two days before we were due to be evicted I had a fight with one of the men in the house, throwing him to the ground and kicking him, in my paranoid state thinking that he putting his arm around me to comfort me was actually an attempt at rape. I ran from the house crying and jumped on the train, not knowing where I was going or what I was going to do. I found the building that the Socialist Party had used as the centre for their operations, the building that I had happily walked into at age 15, a time that seemed thousands of years away. I walked up the stairs, hoping to find the door to the roof open, but not knowing why. The door was closed and I desperately ran down the many stairs and out into the street. I found a pay phone and dialled the only number that came into my head, Maud and Kharen from Somebody's Daughter Theatre. They were not home, so I left a message and caught the train back to my own house in Richmond. I do not remember what I said in that message but about five minutes after I got home they turned up, took one look at the squalid conditions and said 'We're getting you out of here.' They took me to their house and patiently listened to me explaining that I was perfectly fine but that there was something fundamentally wrong with the universe. Their house was the complete opposite to the one I was being evicted from and I was instantly cheered by their beautifully decorated home. I went to the bathroom and turned on the shower, then looked at myself in the full-length mirror, the first time I'd looked in a mirror in months. I was incredibly thin, my hair was dirty and I was struck by the fact that I had no breasts to speak of. I stood under the shower for ages, feeling eternally grateful to Maud and Kharen and wondering where I was going to go from here.

It was decided that I needed to stop doing drugs and, by that stage, I could see Maud and Kharen's point. I was far from happy and had about $50 to my name. I could not move into a share-house without money for a security deposit. Anyway, living in Melbourne probably wasn't a good idea as I was likely to go and buy more drugs. Maud and Kharen knew a woman who ran a camp and organic farm in the country. She often took in people who had drug problems or had just got out of jail. They called her and she said I could stay there for as long as I needed to. We packed my few possessions and my cat, Sensei, into Maud's little car and drove for two hours until we came to the farm. The landscape was amazing with mountains and mountain ash trees, which Maud told me were the second tallest type of tree in the world after the giant redwoods from America. I felt like I needed a joint, but I had promised Maud I would not smoke any more and was determined to keep my word, seeing that she and Kharen had saved me from a nasty situation. We were greeted by the woman who ran the farm, Robyn. She looked to be in her fifties and radiated energy and enthusiasm. She showed me to a cabin at the back of the camp and I did my best to settle in. The farm was host to a group of people called Willing Workers on Organic Farms, or Woofers for short. Two of the Woofers were staying in the cabin next to mine – two schoolgirls on their holidays. They were very friendly and I soon struck up a conversation with them. The first night I was there, I got into my bed and started talking to the younger Woofer who pointed out an enormous huntsman spider inches from my face. She grabbed my sketchbook and killed the spider for me and I thanked her profusely, knowing I could not have slept in the cabin knowing that it was there. The next day I convinced Robyn to let me stay in her office and sleep on the couch, terrified the huntsman may have a mate lurking in the wardrobe in my cabin.

The farm was home to many animals – a sheep called Mintie who had a frightening habit of butting anyone it didn't like, usually when they were sitting next to the camp fire, a cow, Lovey, who was 20 years old and very friendly, as well as six horses and a dog who was supposed to be a mother for guide dog puppies, but who usually mated with the mutt from the next farm, leaving Robyn to have to find homes for the many puppies. Robyn was also a wildlife carer and took in injured native animals. There were wombats and kangaroos, parrots, magpies and occasionally vicious and grumpy koalas, one of which bit through

Robyn's finger and broke the bone. Robyn had to get up every two hours during the night to feed the tiny baby animals and would take the older animals that were strong enough for a three-mile run each morning at 5 am After a couple of weeks staying at the farm I was amazed to hear that Robyn was 70 years old.

I didn't have to pay any rent to live at the farm but was expected to work for my bed and board and was soon helping to cook the meals for campers, cleaning out cabins and looking after a baby wallaby. I was relieved that I didn't have to pay any rent as I had very little money; the social security office had stopped paying me as I hadn't put in the form I was supposed to. For a while I was the only person with 'problems' that lived at the farm but soon another girl arrived, a tough 16-year-old called Kerry who had nowhere to go. She knew a lot about horses and had promised to help Robyn look after the six that were on the property. Kerry claimed she was a lesbian but, thankfully, was not very interested in me. She played little games, liking somebody one day and hating them the next. I never knew where I stood with her and was constantly confused when in her company. She was also a dope-smoker and soon we were smoking together. Robyn told her I was not supposed to smoke dope and so she started using this as a weapon against me. Kerry would tell me she had some dope and that I could have some, then all of a sudden change her mind. I never knew what was going on and could not understand why Kerry was so mean. If I thought she was mean to me, though, that left no word to describe her treatment of the next young homeless person who moved in, Rikki. Rikki was 15, had a child and was often suicidal. Kerry would talk loudly about how she wanted to stab Rikki, loud enough for the poor girl to hear. She told her she didn't take 'real' overdoses and that she should 'do it properly'. Then one day Kerry started being nice to Rikki and sharing her drugs with the younger girl. I only ever took what people said and did on face value and found Kerry a nightmare to be around.

I was making a lot of art on the farm, most of it quite dark and sombre, but some of the people who came to work on the farm bought a couple of my paintings and this encouraged me to keep working. I had pride in my ability as an artist and my new role on the farm, house cook. I was in charge of feeding all the workers and residents and I took my job very seriously. I would try out a new recipe every couple of days and everyone liked the results. For the first time in what seemed forever I had a job to do and people who appreciated my efforts. I wanted to make a go of things here at the farm and had found a new surrogate parent, Robyn. I talked to Robyn as I had my mother when I was a teenager. I confided in her about everything and was happy just knowing I could talk to her. The only thing I didn't tell her was my increasingly frequent dope-smoking sessions with Kerry and the fact that I was feeling the same mad way I had when I left the drug-dealer's house in Richmond.

There was a young Aboriginal man living at the farm called Tom. I liked Tom, who was gentle and quiet and loved telling stories of his travels around Australia. I confided in him my deepening feelings of depression and he listened, telling me not to do anything to hurt myself but to talk to him if I needed help. I felt bad about talking to Tom though, and didn't want to worry him with my problems. A couple of days after we spoke, I cut my wrists, not doing any major damage, but just wanting to feel pain. Tom came into my room and found me. He promised not to tell anyone, but the next day I found his room empty – he had moved out, off for another adventure travelling around Australia. I felt so guilty and thought myself responsible for his having left. The guilt only served to make me feel worse about myself. I took an overdose of another of the residents' epilepsy medication and ended up in general hospital; then, for the first time in my life, was committed to a psychiatric institution.

7 .

Watching the End of the World

I arrived at the psychiatric hospital in an ambulance. I'd spent the trip there chatting with the ambulance officers, unaware that I was there involuntarily and had no say in the situation. When I got to the hospital I was met by a nurse who had three fingers missing on one hand and two missing on the other. I was struck by the fact that I was being treated by someone who wasn't quite 'whole' and thought this a little unjust. The nurse, whose name I later learned was Richard, handed me a pamphlet on the rights of committed, or involuntary, patients. I freaked out at the thought I might be here for years and punched him. Although he had less fingers than most, he was quite strong and wrestled me to the ground. I spent the next few days in the seclusion unit with no one for company but myself and a nurse in a glass cubicle who didn't want to talk to me at all. I was lonely and bored and, knowing nothing about modern psychiatric hospitals, had no idea of how long I was going to be in there. My only point of reference was the film *One Flew Over the Cuckoo's Nest*, which didn't exactly inspire confidence in the hospital authorities.

After a couple of days, Maud and Kharen came up from Melbourne to visit me. They had brought me some fantastic presents: a box of pastels and nice paper and a white silk shirt. I loved the feel of the silk shirt and held it up to my face to feel its softness. The pastels were soon put to work on some drawings, although I had to convince the nurses to let me have them.

I had not spoken to my parents in six months, the last time being the time I called and thought my mum had hung up on me, but I finally plucked up the courage and called them from the hospital. To my surprise they were delighted to hear from me. They told me they had thought I'd died. I assured them I was not dead and we chatted for ages, me telling them of the many things that had happened since the last time we spoke, this time being honest about what I had really been doing while living in my drug-addled household in Richmond. My mum told me I was welcome to stay with them whenever I wanted to and I was relieved. She assured me that she had not hung up on me that Saturday morning all those months ago but that the pay phone had been faulty. Feeling like an idiot I apologised for not calling her. I was glad to once again have a relationship with my parents and intended to visit them whenever I could.

After a few days I was let out of seclusion and allowed to mix with the rest of the patients. They seemed a depressing bunch and would burden me with their many problems. I tried hard to pretend I cared but in reality I just wanted them to leave me alone. The atmosphere of the place was dismal and instilled in me a tragic feeling. The door was usually locked and we were only allowed out occasionally. I became quite a star among the patients, telling my stories of jail and drugs. It seemed that no one there had ever met such an exciting young woman. There was one patient who bothered me, though. A young boy of 15 called Warren who was said to have Asperger Syndrome, as I had been told I did, a fact I had not divulged to any of the psychiatrists at the hospital due to my state of denial. Warren was very similar to myself at his age and was always immersed in some book or another. He had no qualms about telling people exactly what he thought and one day chastised me for smoking, saying it caused cancer. I threatened him with something or another and continued smoking, but deep down I hated him for being so like my worst vision of myself. I had become the opposite of him and I wanted it to stay that way. I told no one of my diagnosis in prison by the psychologist, Vicki Batista, and the doctors told me instead that I was schizophrenic, a conclusion I was a lot happier to live with than the scary truth.

Although on admission I had thought I would be in the hospital for years, they actually let me go after about three weeks and I was sent back to the farm with Robyn and the animals. I was given medication for psychosis and depression but it didn't make me feel any better. I did, however, get quite obsessive about taking it, thinking if I did not I would go completely crazy and kill myself, or worse, someone else. I had been told not to smoke any more dope or I really would go mad, yet while I was extremely diligent about taking my medication, I had no intention of taking people's advice about marijuana very seriously. I liked drugs; they made me feel good (or at least numb) and I could not imagine life without them. Kerry and I smoked bongs together when she was speaking to me, and when she was not I fantasised about the large quantities of dope she said she could get hold of, looking forward to the day we would be on speaking terms again.

I had made friends with a man who lived two towns away who sold leather belts and dog collars in the city at a market – Pete. Pete had been a member of a motorcycle gang in his youth and still played hard when he got the chance, smoking dope and drinking whisky. Pete had seven cats, three horses and a dog and lived so far out of town that the electricity was not connected and he had to use a car battery if he wanted to watch TV or listen to the radio. I loved going to his house, drinking too much and patting the large number of available cats. His horses would try to eat my jacket in a show of affection and he would tell me stories of the old days in the bikie gang. He was growing a hallucinogenic peyote cactus and had promised me some of it. I anticipated the maturing of this cactus with glee, imagining patting cats while 'tripping', not thinking of its detrimental effects on my mental health.

I never got to try the peyote though – I had a huge fight with Kerry and had to move out, not wanting to stay in the vicinity of someone who scared me as much as she did. Kerry was smoking dope; I could smell it wafting out from under her door. I went in to ask for a smoke, but as I entered her room she hid the bong and told me there was no dope. I went and told Robyn that Kerry was smoking drugs and not offering me any, thinking this was bound to make her share her stash with me. Unfortunately Robyn didn't take to the idea that Kerry was smoking in her house and had a go at her. Kerry threatened to kill me and I was so scared I stayed in the house with Robyn, worried that Kerry might make good her threat. The next day I knew I had to get out of there and saw that I had two options: move to Melbourne and back to my old life, or call my parents and see if they would let me stay with them. I chose the latter option and my mum and dad drove the five-hour trip to Robyn's farm and collected me.

Relieved as I was to have somewhere to go, I was not at all sure that moving back home was such a good idea as I was very different from my parents and had lived out of home for four years. When my parents got to Robyn's farm and helped me pack up my things, my mum was very concerned about some bedding I'd lost somewhere in my travels. I was irritated by this as, to me, a quilt was just a thing, not as important as a person, or even a cat, and it mattered very little. I thought my mum's complaints were very petty and wished I'd lost some more of the things she'd given me, just to annoy her. One thing I didn't have to take with me, unfortunately, was my beloved cat, Sensei. Sensei had loved living in the country and, after a week or so of hiding in the cupboard, had made friends with all the animals in the neighbour-hood. Her best mate was a wombat who she would follow under the house. I never worried about Sensei, thinking she was as streetwise a cat as I had ever met, but while I was in hospital a terrible thing happened. Sensei picked a fight with a big mother possum who was protecting her young. The possum bit Sensei on the neck and she died instantly. I found out when I was in the hospital after having tried to kill myself. The uncanny link between my cat and me had ended in her death and I felt responsible. For the first time in my life I felt loss at the death of another. I would wake in the morning expecting Sensei to come in for a pat and she would not be there. It was like I'd lost a part of myself and I would have given anything to have my best friend back, the cat that I'd had for four years and who had loved me dearly. One of the first things I asked my parents on arriving at their farm was if I could have a little cat to keep me company. The girl next door had a cat that had just had kittens and, after many justified complaints from my parents about the damage cats can do to the native environment, I was allowed to take one of the kittens home with me. I called my kitten Monty after both Monty Python and my dad's nickname for her, Montezuma, possibly given her for her habit of zooming through the crops to get a pat from him. She was to live in the shed and be my new feline best friend.

It was strange moving in with my parents after so long away from them and I took some time to get adjusted. I loved my parents but that didn't necessarily mean I liked them all that much. I set about making friends with my dad – something I would have thought impossible a few years previously but which now seemed like a good idea. I learned a lot about my dad in a very short period of time. He was not the ogre my socialist teenager self had thought him, but a sensitive, kind, gentle man who had a great (if slightly rude) sense of humour. When I lived at home the second time I had few of the arguments that had marked my relationship with my dad in my teens; rather, I had conversations with him. My mum was at work most of the time and I only saw her in the evenings and on weekends. I found myself wanting her company a lot of the time and looked forward to our nightly games of Scrabble and hair-brushing sessions. I developed quite a taste for Scrabble and became an expert. I'd practise playing against myself and try to beat my previous high scores. My best for each hand was around 400 points and I was soon giving my mum, the reputed Purkis Scrabble Queen, a run for her money.

I had a serious financial issue in that the social security office had not paid me for over three months and I had been living off the last dole cheque I had received for all that time, thanking my lucky stars that I was living rent-free. I was happy living in the moment and was unconcerned that I hadn't been paid a cent since the previous October but my mum and dad thought I needed some money to get by and help with the bills and so on. My parents took me off to the social security office and I was given the relevant forms to apply for a disability pension. On my first try for this benefit I was refused but after a furious phone call to the office supervisor from my mum and an appeal I was granted the pension. I was also back-paid for the last three months and suddenly had $2500 in my bank account. While in my incarnation as a drug addict I had not cared about saving money, I was now overjoyed at my instant savings account and was determined to make some use of my new-found wealth. I set about buying all the things I had wanted in the previous few months: books, CDs, new 'Doc Marten' boots and nice sculptures and paintings for my bedroom. I also paid my parents $50 each week for board and supplemented my contribution to the household by cooking dinner every night.

I was not the innocent being I had been the last time I had lived at home and my parents did their best to take this into account. I was allowed to drink alcohol, and even to smoke cigarettes, providing I went outside to do it. I lived a fairly carefree and independent life at home and, although it was a bit lonely having the house all to myself when my mum was at work and my dad was out on the farm, I soon settled into a routine and got very used to living at home again. I read books as I never had before, enjoying Isabel Allende, William S. Burroughs and my favourite, Jack Kerouac. I would buy a new book every time I was paid my pension and soon had quite a collection. I also bought many CDs and my music collection gradually grew to include all the bands I loved, mainly grunge groups like Nirvana, Jane's Addiction and Sonic Youth. For the first time in a long while I actually felt happy and content. I felt I could make a life for myself here on the farm.

I still had a substance abuse problem but was doing my best to limit its effects. I would buy a large bottle of spirits, usually tequila or Bundaberg rum, and get drunk once a week. Both my parents thought this was the lesser of all the possible evils and I soon got used to spending every Wednesday night getting sloshed in the company of my parents. I tried to the best of my ability to avoid marijuana but it was a hard task and soon I was smoking again. I kept my drug use secret from my parents and would roll a joint long after they had gone to bed and smoke it in my bedroom, with a towel under the door to stop the smoke escaping into the rest of the house. I was amazed that my secret smoking was never discovered, although it came very close a few times. One night I was watching the all-night music video programme in a thoroughly stoned state and, at about 4 am, my dad came in. We had a conversation, my heart pounding at a million miles an hour. I was sure he knew that I was stoned, but it seemed he did not as it was never mentioned. Another time I had smoked some bongs with the girl next door while my parents were at church. When they returned they found her and me staring at my newly-bought Pakistani rug, with the heater up as high as it would go and all the doors open. My parents asked me suspiciously what we were doing and if we were 'trying to heat the whole house!' I replied that we were just admiring my new rug.

I was in contact with a fellow ex-student from RMIT, Arthur, and he had invited me to come and stay with him in Melbourne for a few days. I knew that the visit would include lots of dope-smoking sessions and withdrew some money from the bank with which to replenish my stash; my supply was running thin.

Arthur had a girlfriend, Sally, and when I stayed they were in the process of breaking up. It was a very uncomfortable situation and I wished they had gotten it over with before I had arrived so I didn't have to put up with their bickering. The minute I arrived Arthur passed me a bong and I smoked it, followed by several more. Sally came in with three bottles of wine and complained that Arthur smoked all day every day. I thought the reason they were having relationship trouble must be that Arthur smoked dope and Sally drank wine and that their reliance on different substances made them incompatible. I marvelled at Arthur's collection of underground magazines and comics and his impressive music collection. We smoked all night and when I awoke the next day I was still as stoned as I had been the night before.

During my visit my old friends Lee and Sharon came over for dinner. I was ashamed of myself for being stoned when they arrived, knowing one of the reasons I had been asked to leave their house had been my prolific dope habit and that they probably thought I was a terminal addict. Trying to sober up, I offered Lee a drawing I had done the week before, which he accepted and promptly displayed upside-down. At dinner we drank five bottles of wine between the five of us and Arthur and I smoked many bongs. I was too wasted to carry on a sensible conversation and felt completely embarrassed. I stocked up on drugs the next day, marvelled at the pretty coloured foils the deals were wrapped in, stuck the deals in my new Doc Martens and caught the train home, to where my parents were waiting.

I thought I needed to have an exhibition of my new artworks and contacted the local artists' cooperative in a nearby town. They liked my work and offered me a show the coming November, eight months away. I set about making as many drawings as I could and now had something to work towards. I was drawing little landscapes in pastel mainly from imagination. They did not really have much behind them in terms of ideas, but they were visually very attractive and people would comment to me about how much they liked these drawings. I was also making self-portraits on a regular basis and, while they were still scary-looking, they did not have the bleakness of the ones I had done while living on the farm with Robyn. I took over the spare bedroom and made it into a studio. I would work until late in the evening and took great pride in my art. My show was going to be a huge success, I just knew it. I happily invited people to my upcoming exhibition, even though it was many months away.

After much deliberation, my parents decided to build a self-contained unit on their farm that I could live in. I helped with some of the design decisions and did my best to help with the construction. My parents told me that people with Asperger Syndrome often lived with their parents all their life and, while I didn't want to hear about something I had convinced myself I did not have, the idea of living with my mum and dad forever certainly appealed to me. The little treats I bought for myself every pay day were soon focused on the new home being built for me. I was going to have an artist's house, filled with trinkets and sculptures and beautiful things, much as my socialist friends George and Julie's house had been. For the first time ever I was to have somewhere that was exclusively *mine* and I was so proud and pleased and full of love for my so-generous parents I could not imagine ever being sad again. My dad's friend from England, Rodney, who had witnessed my freshly-shaved head years previously, had come for another visit and I was determined to get along with him so that my parents could see how mature and sensible I could be. To my amazement Rodney and I got along quite well, although he was a little too interested in me for my liking. I accompanied Rodney on a tour of the local vineyards and tasted wines with him, I went with him to a town he thought sounded like an interesting place because of its name, 'Burrumbuttock'. It was really just a one-horse town with a pub and a post office. Rodney was very disappointed, having perhaps expected some reference to what he thought was the town's hilarious name, but he took a photo of the main street anyway. All four of us went for a driving holiday together and visited Canberra and some coastal towns in New South Wales. I spent the trip looking for shops that sold beautiful and sparkly things with which I could decorate my new house when it was finished. I loved semi-precious stones and amassed a large collection of pretty rocks that I loved to stroke and lick or just rub against my face. We stopped at a motel in a town just outside of Canberra and I started looking through my mum's bag for her purse just for something to do. I came across a prison visitor's card and assumed it was for me until I read the name of the prisoner being visited. It was not my name on the card but that of my old partner-in-crime, Joe. I had never felt so betrayed in my life and accused my parents of every awful thing I could think of, from being disloyal to me to being in collusion with criminals. They informed me that as Christians they had an obligation to love all God's children including people society had discarded. I yelled and screamed in our motel room and seriously considered just walking out into the night to an unknown fate, but eventually calmed down and tried to accept this betrayal. I no longer felt the same way about my parents and started once again to think of them in terms of their authoritative presence and their power over me.

Although I was working on my upcoming exhibition, I felt a need to do something that paid money or at least gave me the opportunity to move into some paid work. My parents had suggested I talk to a drug counsellor at the hospital where my mum worked and do some volunteer work with the residents of the nursing home for the rest of the day I was there, so I started going into work with my mum on the last Friday of each month. I was nervous about the prospect of seeing a counsellor and of starting what I thought was an important and responsible job at the hospital, but after my first day I found I enjoyed both my sessions with Martin, my counsellor, and the work in the old people's home. This generally consisted of me cleaning up and setting the table for lunch and sometimes talking to the residents, most of whom were suffering from dementia and had no idea of where they were or who I was or why we were there at all. I had once again begun to inhabit more than one world. I was now a dutiful daughter co-existing with a tough, drug-using ex-criminal. These worlds were pretty much mutually exclusive and I found myself thinking in two distinct ways a lot of the time. On my first day at the hospital I found a pad of blank prescriptions in a doctor's office that I was cleaning and thought it would be a wonderful thing to steal it and write myself scripts for all the drugs I wanted, but then felt so guilty at having even considered this that I had to tell my mum about the idea. When I worked in the nursing home I was responsible, diligent and sweet Jeanette who would not even think of doing anything against 'the rules' and when I was with my drug counsellor, Martin, I was the 'bad girl' and revelled in telling stories of all the drinking and drugging I had got up to in the previous month. Martin suggested I go to Narcotics Anonymous meetings but I was scared to. I preferred to live in denial of my drug issues and not admit to myself that there was a problem. The closest I got to going to a meeting was the one time I talked to the organiser of the meetings and this encounter challenged and exposed me so much I gave up even considering going to one. Martin also worried me by informing me that recovering addicts could not even have one drink or one joint for the rest of their life and explained that, as a recovering alcoholic, he had not had a drink in many years. I was very attached to being 'off my face', and the idea that I could never again get drunk or stoned was too much for me to cope with. I had a soft spot for Martin, though, and wanted to please him and to stop him worrying about me. I started downplaying and even lying about the amount of drugs or drink I'd taken the previous month so that he would not be so concerned about me.

The volunteer work in the nursing home had filled me with a desire to study nursing and get a job in a hospital, maybe working with older people. I thought I had no chance of being accepted into a nursing course given the fact that I hadn't studied the subjects I needed to gain entry and that I was a drug addict who had been in prison relatively recently. I was given some hope by my mum's boss telling me that the hospital had one of the last on-the-job training courses for nurses and that, given my enthusiasm for my volunteer job and the fact that I had shown I was responsible, my criminal record need not be as big a problem as it might seem. For a while I was determined to become a nurse and spoke at length to my parents about the possibility of working in the hospital, looking after people and being a responsible and respectable member of the community. After a while I realised I would find it incredibly hard to nurse anyone who had mental health problems, had attempted suicide or, worse still, had a diagnosis of autism or Asperger Syndrome. I lost my enthusiasm for nursing pretty quickly after that.

I had signed up with the government's rehabilitation service, free to those on a disability pension as I was. I had every intention of finding a career that would be suitable and, after many questionnaires and tests, I decided I wanted to work with animals. My case worker lined up a voluntary position with the local veterinary hospital. I was going to study to be a veterinary nurse, a low-paid but rewarding career that I considered myself capable of doing. I worked two days a week at the hospital and my duties mainly included taking dogs for a walk and cleaning cages, but sometimes I was allowed to hold the cats and dogs for the vet and to watch operations. I loved my job and thought it was a career I could be happy doing. I was so dedicated at work that I would not smoke a cigarette at all during my eight-hour day and I only took 10 or 15 minutes for lunch. I found it hard to relate to the other employees anyway and preferred the company of the dogs and cats to their human carers. The vets all said I had a natural affinity with animals and I would make an excellent veterinary nurse. There was another young woman working at the veterinary hospital as a volunteer and she spent most of her days smoking and chatting, obviously thinking that if they weren't paying her she might as well not put too much effort into the job. I, on the other hand, took my position as seriously as the CEO of a major company might – I worried if I did anything wrong, I was always on time and I never questioned the tasks I was given by the vets and other nurses. After my six-week voluntary work-trial was finished I was told I should apply for a paid position in a couple of months. I was delighted and thought I would love to be a veterinary nurse and live with my parents for the rest of my days.

While I was doing my volunteer work, I was preparing for a trip to visit my relatives in England – something I looked forward to with both excitement and anxiety. My parents, my mum's friend from church, Mrs McDonald, and I were to travel to the UK for four weeks and visit my grandmother, my aunts and uncles and my six cousins. Dean was not coming, probably because I was unable to spend any time in his company without getting an attack of jealousy, insecurity and hatred and accusing him of being the reason for all my problems. I called him 'Mr Perfect' on several occasions and thought he was the 'good one' who could do no wrong and I was the 'bad one' who did everything wrong. As we left for the airport, I tied a plait in my half-blonde, half-purple hair and said to my parents that it was there to remind me of 'who I was' in what I saw as the invasive company of my formidable English relatives. I was terrified that my relatives, especially my two aunts, would try to make me into someone I was not. For the second time I could remember I spent 30 hours inside a jumbo jet getting increasingly irritated by my parents. I tried to draw on the plane, but found that almost impossible and resigned myself to listening to my favourite grunge music on my Walkman.

England surprised me. I had not remembered it as being so moist and green or the countryside as being so cultivated and dainty. I thought the vibrant green everywhere was amazing and started making drawings, not in the Australian colours I had been using while in that country, but in the greens and greys of the English countryside and sky. Everything seemed very ordered, something that I found difficult to deal with. If somebody had a wild, unplanned garden they were seen as being 'odd'. My aunt Margaret seemed to me to be concerned with things that no serious socialist would ever care about – property values, what the neighbours thought and the like. I did my best to be polite but felt resentful and angry most of the time, having to hold my tongue to keep from offending everyone. I thought the architecture and history of England were wonderful though, and marvelled at the tiny pubs, which seemed to have a million times the atmosphere of their Australian counterparts and were like little homes for the people who came in to drink and chat. The village where my aunt and uncle lived was a source of fascination too, with its ancient church and rickety shops that looked like they were going to tumble into the street at any moment. My aunt informed me that they had been there since the sixteenth century, so I figured they probably had a few years left in them yet.

My uncle Mike was a scientist and a thinker. He seemed to consider everything for a while before he actually said it and I thought him the most intellectual person I had ever met. He knew all the Latin names of plants and would walk through the fields, telling me what family or genus a plant was from and what its correct name was in Latin. I did my best to learn the names of the orchids and other little plants we came across in our travels. Uncle Mike was the one relative I'd met who I desperately wanted to please and for whom I had an enormous amount of respect. I was somewhat judgemental of my other aunts and uncles, thinking them snobs and 'bourgeois' of the worst sort. One night we had dinner at the local hotel with all the family; even my grandma was there, having made the journey from her home in Torquay, a long way for a 93-year-old lady. I was starting to be a bit more 'myself', and anyway was unaware that my relatives would think me a bad person; after all it was two years since my arrest for armed robbery. I made a comment about a drug dealer I knew and some of his doings and my aunt Jean called me 'wicked'. All my insecurities and anxieties rushed out in an angry, defensive outburst. I thought I was not respected for who I was and the life I had lived and that I was being accused of wrongdoing by someone who had not seen me in 11 years who knew nothing about me. I was hurt because deep down I believed what my aunt had said about me, that I was a wicked child who didn't follow the rules. I deserved her condemnation, but I did not let her in on what I thought, preferring to accuse her, and anyone who agreed with her, of intolerance and bigotry.

I began to feel trapped in England; unable to be myself or say what I thought. My parents had pretty much accepted me for what I was a long time ago, but my relatives in England seemed to me a little judgemental and I became increasingly sensitive to everything they said to me. I scanned their words for sarcasm, judgement or intolerance and saw those things in most of what they said even if they weren't there. While I was trying my best to do what I thought was expected of me, my past seemed to linger around me and colour everyone's opinions of me. I desperately wanted to go back to my largely happy life at my parents' farm, where it was just the three of us and I could be myself. I noticed that the braid I had tied in my hair to signify my individuality had come undone on the plane on the way to England and to me that meant I had been compromised. I was no longer free to be myself in the presence of the family members whose beliefs and judgements meant so much to me. I liked being in a different and interesting country but I wished I could go and do my own thing and maybe meet some people my age who didn't spend their Sundays in church. I thought Christians a bunch of judgemental, thoughtless, right-wing people who rarely practised what they preached and could only enjoy the magnificent cathedrals and village chapels we visited by looking at them in architectural and art-historical terms. I was determined to avoid Christians as much as I could when I returned to Australia and looked forward to my return to the security of my world at home. I went through the motions of being an honoured guest from so far away and of attending family gatherings and dinners, but inside I longed to go home and felt myself liking England less and less with each day that passed.

When I finally returned home I felt particularly proud of myself, having not smoked marijuana for several weeks. I'd finally admitted my secret dope-smoking to my parents and had sadly thrown my remaining few crumbs of grass in the bin, much to my parents' delight. The pressure of keeping this enormous secret from my parents was much harder, I thought, than the difficulties I may encounter should I stop smoking. I had phoned the manager of a local veterinary clinic and had arranged a work trial, my art exhibition was fast approaching and I had hundreds of little pastel drawings to exhibit. The flat my parents were building for me was almost finished and I had decided to start having therapy for the sexual abuse I had experienced in my past. Everything was going so well for me; I would soon have a job, a house, an exhibition to add to my somewhat pitiful artist's resumé and I was hopefully going to get some relief from the problems caused me by some of the less pleasant incidents from my past.

Three weeks after returning from England I awoke in the early hours of the morning feeling that something was not right at all. I sat in the dark for a while, feeling more and more depressed as the time went on and finally decided to wake my mum. As the morning light crept into the sky I went from sanity to madness. I was unable to speak, I hated myself and wanted to die and I knew, with every certainty, that the world was coming to an end very, very soon. My mum drove me to the local psychiatric hospital, not knowing what was wrong with me, but realising I was going through something very bad. As she explained what had happened to the doctors I stood outside, smoking a cigarette and pushing the lit end into my hand, not feeling the pain. The nurses tried to speak to me and I just looked at the ground, unable to communicate. I remember them asking my mum if I could speak, but as far as I was concerned I could not speak and never wanted to again. I was admitted to the hospital, this one much more modern than the one I had been in the year before, with private rooms for patients rather than dorms, and freshly-painted walls. I was told I was to stay there until I got better.

I thought that white people were all evil and were responsible for all the problems of the world. I only wanted to speak to people who were not white. I spent my time with an Aboriginal girl who was a patient. She had been a drug addict years before and it had left her with schizophrenia. We listened to music together and played board games. I found I felt better if I painted and managed to produce a series of terrifying paintings depicting the end of the world, something I thought was imminent. I soon ended up in the seclusion room as I used anything I could to hurt myself, wanting to express what was inside me but being unable to communicate my distress verbally or emotionally. I thought I was in prison and the nurses were evil guards who wanted me dead so I tried to escape to freedom and safety by running through the nurses' station into the main ward beyond. The nurses thought I was being violent and aggressive for the sake of it and gave me huge quantities of Largactyl, an anti-psychotic drug that had been in use since the middle of the twentieth century. They gave me so much of this drug that I developed low blood-pressure so badly I could not stand up and had to lie on the floor with my feet elevated. The drugs did not help with my psychotic thoughts but did mean that I was too drowsy and slow to do much damage to myself or the nursing staff.

After a month I was discharged from the hospital and returned to my parents' farm, this time with the diagnosis of 'psychotic depression' and a prescription for antidepressants and Largactyl. The doctors let me go home a day after I had been let out of the seclusion ward and I was far from well, although my belief that the world was coming to an end had mostly disappeared and I no longer thought white people responsible for all the evils of the world. I had become obsessed with hurting myself though, and found the habit impossible to break. As I had almost no ability to understand how what I did affected others, I paid no attention to my parents' concern for me or their horror at what I was doing to myself. I couldn't see that they were constantly worried about what I might do and I never tried to communicate how I felt to them, apart from to tell them that I felt like hurting myself. My depression coupled with my lack of empathy was a dangerous combination and it wasn't long before I was back in hospital, this time in the town where we used to go to church years before.

This hospital was the last remaining wing of a nineteenth-century insane asylum that had been marked for closure. The first week I spent at this hospital was spent in the seclusion room with the door shut. I was determined to get the attention of the nurses who seemed to want to ignore me. I stripped naked in the room and waited for them to come in and tell me off. I ran against the wall until they came in and told me not to. I yelled and screamed and threatened, hoping someone would come and rescue me from the despair I felt constantly. I felt that I could not be happy ever again living the life I was and started to try to remember times I had been happy, wanting to relive them and put myself in the same situation I had been in then. One period stood out in my life when I thought I had been genuinely happy – my time as a prisoner in Fairlea, 17 months previously. I knew what I had to do; I needed to get arrested for some crime and go back to jail. I was sure I had been happy when I was in prison. I'd had friends, I was popular and, most of all, I'd fitted in. The outside world was hard, but prison simply involved following a set of rules and doing what was expected of one. I had to go back to jail and I thought I knew just how to get there.

I still had a suspended sentence hanging over my head so theoretically all I had to do to go to prison was to commit an offence that carried a *possible* prison sentence. I didn't have to rob a bank or kill anyone; all I had to do was punch someone, not necessarily hard, and wait for them to make a police report. While I didn't feel particularly strongly about the nurses one way or another and certainly didn't think them deserving of physical violence, my desire to get locked up again was so strong that I didn't really care about how the nurses would feel and started attacking them on a regular basis. The doctors thought I might have some form of epilepsy that caused me to be unable to control violent impulses and sent me off for tests, only to discover that was not the case. I did not communicate my wish to go to prison to the nurses so they were left completely mystified as to why I was treating them so badly. I was getting a bit impatient at their lack of willingness to report my acting out to the police and stepped up my campaign of random aggression. Eventually I attacked the head doctor, a man who seemed a lot less concerned when I was attacking nurses but took my attempt to punch him considerably more seriously and called the police. I was relieved and thought that soon I would be happy again, as I had been two years before, in prison with criminals who would understand me and like me.

While all this violence and aggression was going on, my art exhibition was due to go up and I felt completely unprepared to do anything about it. Somehow I managed to get a day out from the hospital to install my many drawings and to attend the exhibition opening. It seemed that everyone I knew who lived in the area had come along to support my show and for the first time in ages I almost felt happy. A couple of people I knew from Somebody's Daughter Theatre had come up from Melbourne, one of them giving the opening speech. An art critic from a Melbourne newspaper turned up and called my show 'The most exciting exhibition by a young artist I've seen in a long time' and I felt very proud of myself indeed. My works sold almost instantly and before long I realised I'd made over $1000 just on the opening night. Had I been in a better frame of mind I would have been overjoyed. Had I not been so determined to go to prison my success might have given me a reason to lift myself out of the hole I found myself in. However, I had my mind set on going to prison and didn't take much notice of how good I felt when the art critic was praising my work or when I realised that I'd sold a large proportion of my drawings. I returned to the hospital, my black mood returning the moment I stepped inside the door. Two days later I attacked another nurse and this time it meant the police arrived instantly and charged me with assault. I went to court and was refused bail. I was going back to prison. I thought that surely this had to mean I was going to be happy again.

8 .

Dying and Surviving

I spent 11 days in the discomfort of the local police watch-house, real-ising as the days passed that I was no happier than I had been while at the hospital. I hoped that when I arrived at the women's prison I would finally feel the same way I had when I had been at Fairlea. I had heard that I would not be going to Fairlea this time but to a new prison in the outer suburbs, a privatised prison, made possible by the free-market policies of my old nemesis, State Premier Jeff Kennett. I spent hours fantasising about what this place would look like, who would be there and which officers from Fairlea would be there. I even dreamt of my imagined prison, seeing a modern, well-designed penal institution where it was easy to get away with anything due to the officers being the nicest in the country. I didn't even mind the four-hour trip in an uncomfortable prison van with no windows and metal seats – I was travelling to the place where I would finally no longer be depressed and unhappy. I wouldn't hurt myself again and, by the time I was released, I would be cured.

The new Metropolitan Women's Correction Centre was not the penal paradise of my dreams, rather it was a bleak, drab collection of cheaply-built buildings ranged across a treeless wilderness. While Fairlea had been built in the 1970s, this place had only been around for six months and no one seemed to know what was going on, including the governor – a middle-aged man who had a comb-over hairstyle and thought the prison would be improved with the addition of an assortment of animals. The RSPCA were called in a few months after the introduction of peacocks, donkeys and emus, which were left to roam around in the space between the inner and outer walls of the prison and were undernourished and mistreated. There was mud everywhere and the wind whistled through the place, making it either way too hot or far too cold depending on the weather.

The day I arrived at the Metropolitan Women's Correction Centre (the MWCC for short) I was taken to be processed with three other new arrivals and the process took many hours due to some technical problem with the security system. The head of the medical centre took pity on the four of us and offered us a cup of coffee. Anticipating a delicious, hot cup of sweet coffee I was instead given a cup of coffee to which the nurse-manager had added salt instead of sugar. This just about summed up my initial experiences of the MWCC – I had expected an improvement on my situation but was instead landed in a mismanaged, underfunded and confusing place where the rules changed every few days and a new governor seemed to appear every few months.

I discovered that nobody I had known at Fairlea was in the prison at the time I arrived and so had to get to know a bunch of strangers who did not find me cute and quirky as the older women at Fairlea had. Rather, I was seen as a freak by my new cellmates and before long I had used my prison-issue safety razor to cut myself and found myself in the suicide observation cell. This place was hell as far as I was concerned; the light was left on constantly and there was a camera recording my every move, including my visits to the toilet. I had my period but was not allowed a tampon and was also denied the privilege of underwear, so had to squeeze a pad between my legs constantly. There was nothing to do in this place but wait to be allowed to leave. I did not even have a book. Insects, including spiders, crawled around the walls and I was unable to kill them. The first night I was there the officers left the radio playing through the intercom and then left the unit so I had the Top 40 playing all night and the light on. I got to sleep after hours and hours, after having waking visions of people insulting me and abusing me and hearing their insults as if they were in the next room. When I informed the nurse of these visions the next day she informed me that 'You don't hear voices Purkis. Stop talking crap' and that was that.

After four days in the suicide observation cell I was allowed out and, expecting to return to the unit where I had been before, was most surprised to be taken to another part of the prison. When I asked the officer where he was taking me he informed me that I was going 'somewhere where you'll be safe' and I knew my life as a respected member of the prison community was over; he was taking me to Protection, where informers and child-killers were housed and where you went if you couldn't look after yourself. Once you had been in Protection no one respected you ever again if you entered the mainstream prison population. I pleaded with him not to take me there but it was decided. Resignedly, I asked the screw, Ian, to make sure the prisoners who cleaned out my cell gave me my tobacco, hoping they had not already stolen it. My prison-issue clothes and other belongings soon arrived at my new home, unit A1, and I searched them, looking in vain for the two packets of tobacco I had brought when I first arrived. I spent a week in the protective custody unit hating every moment I was there but thinking the women here were nicer than the girls I had come across before going to the suicide observation cell.

After continuous pleas to join the main population and go back to where I had been originally, I was allowed to return. When I got back to my original unit, however, the atmosphere was far from friendly. The screw, Ian, had accused the cleaners of the unit of stealing my tobacco and they wanted me to pay for it. I had no idea of how to get out of the jam I now found myself in but thought quickly and surmised that if I attacked the screw that would get me out of my sticky situation. I walked into the office, feeling determined, and grabbed the unsuspecting screw by the collar and swung a punch at him. In an instant he had me on the ground and I was handcuffed and thrown back in the suicide observation cell where I spent another five days.

When I finally was allowed back to the unit the two girls who wanted to fight me had been moved to the prison farm and an old friend from Fairlea, Clare, had arrived. I was saved, as far as I was concerned, and, better still, the women who had known I had been in Protection had gone. Criminal Jeanette was well and truly back. I settled into a routine and soon moved to another, much more pleasant unit with some of the women I had known in Fairlea and a few other girls.

I had once again got myself a job in industries, this time weighing little boxes of nuts and bolts and closing the boxes. It was dull work but the pay had increased in my time on the outside and I was now being paid the whopping rate of $6.50 per day. I enrolled in some classes at Education, once again doing drama and art, and started to spend all my free time in the library with my new friend Terri. Terri was an enigma in that she was so right-wing on some issues as to almost be a Nazi. She was extremely racist and a firm believer in white supremacy, something I found particularly offensive. On other issues she was quite liberal-minded and progressive, though. A charismatic woman, Terri had been imprisoned for three years for the attempted murder of another woman. She was quite scary in some respects but she was warm-hearted and generous and cared greatly for prisoners like myself who had mental health problems. Terri would make me nice things in art classes and encourage me to decorate my cell with them. We had as much fun as we could in the situation and talked late into the night in our unit. Terri involved me in something that I regretted for years afterwards, though, the beating of a young woman who Terri had a problem with. Terri, myself and one other girl rounded on this poor girl one night and threatened and menaced her, Terri bashed her and told her if she went to Protection she'd 'pay for it'. After the beating, Terri gave me a nice blanket owned by the young girl and a shirt that belonged to her. I took the things but never wore the shirt and gave away the blanket, not wanting to be tainted with the memory of being part of threatening and intimidating someone who seemed even more scared than me. I did keep the shirt though, and felt increasing amounts of shame each time I looked at the thing.

A short while later I was being walked back to the unit with another girl, Jules, late at night by two screws and one of them started saying rude things about Jules. I turned around and punched the officer who was insulting my friend. This time they took me to the unit that I would spend most of my sentence in – Management. This unit was the same place I had come to on arrival at the MWCC but it had changed. Now there was a locked yard outside the door and an officer attending permanently. Prisoners here were watched day and night and were locked in their cells from 6 o'clock at night to 8.30 in the morning. The problem prisoners were housed here, mainly women who had been caught fighting or using drugs. Prisoners in Management were not allowed to any other part of the prison unless for some valid reason and accompanied by two officers.

I missed my unit and the women who were there and wished I hadn't attacked the officers but I had now got a name for myself as the girl who attacked the screws and, much to my surprise, other prisoners were very wary of me and didn't ever try to give me a hard time. I thought this was quite a good reputation to have in here and I was quite happy to keep up the act. I still had my dual attitude to authority and deep down I really didn't feel any animosity to most of the prison officers, thinking they were actually quite interesting to talk to. On the surface, and to my fellow prisoners, I expressed the opinion that I thought the screws the saddest, most pitiful and 'power-tripping' people on earth but inside I kept wanting to talk to the officers and make friends with them. In Management most prisoners were unemployed and received just $2 per day – not nearly enough for a smoker to buy cigarettes for the week, and hardly enough to keep a prisoner supplied with coffee. I was given the job as the unit's 'billet', the cleaner, and I was relieved to get paid the prison's average pay of $6.50 per day. I had enough to help out friends with cigarettes and coffee and had something to keep me occupied, even if I hated mopping the floors. As billet, I was allowed to stay out of my cell a little longer than the rest of the Management prisoners, so I could make sure everyone had their carton of milk for the night and to give the officer on duty anything the women may have left out so he or she could unlock their cell and give it to them. I also had enough money to hire a TV, the ultimate privilege, and often half the girls in the unit would be crowded around my little TV set watching the soapies, quiz shows or the midday movie.

Most of the time I was in Management my old friend Clare was there also. Unlike me, Clare was the real deal as far as being a tough girl was concerned. I liked her but made sure I never did anything that would upset her and spent a good deal of my time and energy trying to make sure she was happy. She had a power game going with her cup of coffee and would send it back every time anyone made her one, claiming that nobody could get it right. I would happily make coffee or tea for anyone who wanted it, liking to be a good host, and most people would comment that 'You make a good brew, Jeanette' on drinking their cuppa. Clare, however, would never admit that she liked any cup of coffee I made her, always complaining that there was too much sugar, or not enough milk or that it was too hot, or too cold. Clare had been in some institution or another all her life. She was a heroin addict and had learned how to get ahead in the criminal world. I respected her and was grateful for the street-cred hanging around with Clare gave me, but in many of the things she did I thought I saw she was pure evil.

I was surviving in the best way I knew how – acting. Once again I was being and doing exactly what the people around me expected and was amazed that no one ever spotted the scared, nervous and disturbed person that I was. I had a six-month sentence to serve but it seemed to be over very quickly and before long I was walking out the gates to where my parents were waiting to take me to my new home, a boarding house in a dodgy inner suburb known as the drug capital of Melbourne. The boarding house was an old building, built in the nineteenth century. It had 15 rooms and was home to people with mental illnesses, refugees, drug addicts and ex-prisoners like myself. I soon unpacked my boxes of possessions and set about making my tiny room a home. I had some money that the prison had given me on leaving and a little of the money I'd had when living at home with my parents, so I went out and bought something I'd wanted for a long time: a beautiful goose-down quilt complete with Indian-print cover. I had many beautiful bits and pieces bought when I'd lived at home and thought that surrounding myself with these things would surely bring me some good luck. I was still very depressed and had the crisis team from the local hospital visiting me every day to give me my medication. I was on high doses of anti-psychotic drugs, which made me sleepy and slow, but did not make me feel any better about the world. I always wanted to chat to the nurses who visited me, but they never had time to stay.

I didn't like my neighbours very much, they all seemed to be old ladies who thought my music was too loud. One of them even complained about it to the organisation that ran the house, but the girl in the room next to me was my angel. She was younger than me and knew lots of drug dealers. I thought I was onto a good thing and shared the dope I bought with her and let her visit me and listen to music with me sometimes. We would walk together down the main street, the place where all the heroin dealers stood around, asking anyone who looked the part if they were 'chasing?' and not care that it was a dangerous place even during the day, let alone at the hours we were there. The girl, Michelle, took me to another suburb where there were cafes that were fronts for marijuana dealers and we bought a gram deal each, then went home to smoke it.

I was smoking dope by myself one night and another girl knocked on my door, introducing herself as Tamara and saying she had been in prison, too. I chatted with her and her boyfriend and turned around to chop up the dope and roll them a joint. They left after we smoked a few joints together and, after they had gone, I noticed that half of my CDs had gone. They'd been stealing them while I had my back turned. Tamara had claimed the quilt supplied by the boarding house was hers and had taken it with her, me not realising she was lying and that it belonged to the boarding house. I started to think the outside world was not as good as everyone claimed and thought I belonged in prison once more. I was on a community service order and if I didn't comply with its conditions I would be imprisoned again. I cut myself deliberately, just to go to hospital, and, while waiting to be examined, I attacked a prison officer who was there with a male prisoner. I was arrested and refused bail at court. Once more I was going to the MWCC. I had been out of jail for two weeks.

When I arrived at the prison, the officer processing me told me that the new governor wanted to send me to Management as soon as I got there, given my record the last time I had been inside. I was horrified and argued furiously that I had done nothing wrong yet and it would be completely unfair to send me straight to Management. The deputy governor came and spoke to me and I convinced her I would be OK in the mainstream prison population. I would behave and leave the officers and myself alone. A week later I had attacked another officer and was sent to Management, my credibility level with the other inmates at an all-time high and the level the officers trusted me at an all-time low. I was told I would not be let out of the Management Unit for the rest of my three-month sentence and that on top of that I would be prosecuted, not by the internal court system of the prison but by the 'outside court' before a magistrate. It looked like my three months was going to become a much longer time as I had nine charges from attacks on prison officers to face, but I was relieved. I didn't have to worry about coping with life on the outside for a long time; rather, I was back in the safe world of prison where I was told what to do all the time and didn't have to find ways to occupy myself. While I hated the Management Unit on one level, on another it seemed right to me and was more homely than anywhere else I could think of.

A new team of nurses had taken over the running of the medical centre. These ones were all trained psychiatric nurses and each prisoner was allocated a case manager from the medical staff. I was given Laura, a young nurse with a tattoo around her ankle of a garland of roses. She seemed very tough and didn't look like the type of person who tolerated misbehaviour from her charges. I was terrified of her and she took it on herself to cure me of my depression, my self-harm and my aggression through a campaign of rules and 'tough love'. If I hit an officer I had to spend five days in the suicide observation cell with the light on all night and spiders and millipedes for company. If I hurt myself, I got three days in this cell. While I thought her unbearably cruel, she did seem to have my well-being at heart and devised a series of projects to make me happy and give me some hope, the most memorable being the task of writing a five-page document detailing my ultimate goal and how I was to achieve it. I was so depressed at that stage that my only goals were staying in prison for as long as I possibly could, ending up in hospital and perhaps killing myself, so I found this task close to impossible. I knew none of my actual goals were what other people thought were positive and that Laura would be very angry should I write a five-page essay about how I planned to stay in prison as long as possible. Keeping this in mind, I thought about a goal from what seemed the far distant past; I chose the goal of getting a show at the National Gallery of Victoria, the state's huge, publically-funded art gallery that exhibited work by well-known artists from Australia and all over the world. I spent many days staring at the title of my essay wondering how on earth I would be able to write it. After a couple of weeks and having only written one sentence of my five pages, I gave up and threw the thing in the bin. Laura was very disappointed with me and gave me her favourite lecture about how she had been a troubled soul in her younger years and had driven dangerously as a means of self-harm. I hated her all the more and longed for the inevitable change of hands at the medical centre.

During my short stay in the prison's general population I had met a girl who seemed a lot like me in many ways. Katie had black hair, pale skin and a habit of doing as much damage to herself as she possibly could with whatever was handy, up to and including swallowing broken glass and slashing her face. Like me, she was known to the other prisoners as a 'nuff-nuff', a general and not necessarily prejudicial term for someone with any kind of mental health issue. I enjoyed spending time in her company. When I had spent a month or so in the Management Unit, much of it in the suicide observation cell due to my continued attacks on prison officers, Katie turned up, having been sent to Management for her involvement in a riot. Due to the riot, there were not enough cells for each prisoner to have their own cell and Katie was sent to share with me. Two lost souls, we ended up in bed together and spent the next day kissing and hugging. She wrote me a lust poem full of innuendo and outright sexual nastiness and we became girlfriends. As with my love from a few years earlier, I gave no consideration to the possible outcomes of a relationship with such a disturbed person as Katie, and accepted her offer of a relationship without a moment's hesitation. A few weeks later Katie was released and we began a long-distance relationship.

Katie was a true manipulator but I had no way of dealing with this. As I had when dealing with others like her, I took everything she said on face value. I would ring her house from the prison and be unable to contact her for days, getting more and more worried as time went on. When I eventually contacted her, she would inform me of her latest suicidal escapade, including telling me, after being out of contact for two weeks, that she had been standing on a bridge, thinking about jumping but had decided not to. Another time she gleefully told me she'd turned on the gas and shut all the windows. She asked me 'Should I light a cigarette, do you think?' I didn't understand why Katie put me through such hell and hated the fact that she was out there, doing God knows what to herself, while I was in prison and completely unable to do anything but worry. I was convinced that I was in love, because how could I not be in love with someone I worried about so much?

I went to court to face the charges against me from attacking the prison officers and, miraculously, I got out! This eventuality had been foreseen by my concerned parents and the old art teacher from Fairlea. They had arranged for me to stay in a supported accommodation place in the inner city, a house specifically for young lesbians. There were two bedrooms in the house but no other young women were living there so I moved into a house by myself, thinking that maybe this time I could survive in the terrifying world outside the security of prison. I decided I needed to have a cat and went to the local cat shelter to find a new feline companion. I asked the woman at the cat shelter which was the friendliest cat there and she introduced me to Hieronymous, a black and white ball of fluff who started purring the instant she saw me. Without hesitation I paid the $80 for Hieronymous and took her home, amazed at how friendly and sweet she was. I had a CD that Maud and Kharen had given me called *Somebody's Daughter Sings*, a compilation of all the best songs from their theatre productions for the previous 15 years. I listened to this sad CD with my adorable cat.

Nothing in the house seemed to work. The clothes dryer did not turn off and spun all night long, causing the electricity company to send me a bill of $30 for one day's power use. The phone line did not work and I was told I would be without a phone for a week while they fixed it. The TV aerial was faulty, meaning that I had to try and make out the picture from a sea of snow and static. The phone problem was solved by my art teacher friend who loaned me her new mobile phone given her by her work. I had no idea how much mobile calls cost and had a few hour-long conversations with Katie. My cat was good company, but Katie was in psychiatric hospital a long way from where I was and I had no one else to call. After having spent most of the past year in the company of my fellow prisoners, I was now left with just myself and my cat to talk to. I was so lonely I did not know what to do and thought my only options were killing myself or going back to prison. To make matters worse, my cat, Hieronymous, seemed very sick. I thought she was about to die but I was too scared to take her to the vet. I went to my local mental health clinic and threatened the woman behind the counter with a kitchen knife. They called the police and once again I was in custody. This time I had lasted one week in the outside world.

My lawyer told me that he thought I was likely to be sentenced to a long time in prison for my latest crime, maybe even the maximum sentence a magistrate could give me, three years. I secretly hoped that this would be the case and informed him I did not want him to represent me at court and that I would have a go at doing it myself. To my disgust I was only sentenced to three months in prison, the magistrate feeling sorry for me with my mental illness and my wish to defend myself. For the third time I returned to the MWCC and this time was sent straight to the Management Unit. I didn't care though, and felt as bad as I ever had in my life. As I saw it, I had ruined my one chance at happiness and would spend the rest of my life in misery. I had no hope and was filled with a pitiless regret that never seemed to leave me alone. For the first time in my life I genuinely wanted to die and lost any interest in life. I tried to hang myself but failed and ended up in the suicide observation cell once more, but this time I didn't care. The unbearable surroundings seemed fitting and for once I didn't ask at every available opportunity when I would be allowed to go back to my own cell.

When I was finally allowed to my cell I spent most of my time devising ways to die that would be quick enough to escape notice by the screws. I settled on the one way that I thought would work, although looked forward to it with terror as it would be incredibly painful. I spent a while preparing myself and, trembling, held my cigarette lighter to the hem of my pyjamas. Within seconds they were alight and I was going to die. I tried with all my might not to scream, holding on for what seemed eternity and then let out a yell. After another age the officer on duty looked through the tiny window in my cell and unlocked the door as quick as she could. She put out the fire with a towel and I cursed her for saving me. This motherly prison officer had always cared very much about me but I now hated her with everything I had to hate with. I was taken to the medical centre and seen by an old agency nurse with a comb-over who informed me that I just needed to spend the night in the medical centre and I would be able to return to my cell in the morning. Two hours later I was in more pain than I knew was possible and thought that maybe I would die, after all. Then one of the day nurses came in to pick up something they'd left behind after their shift, saw me and called the ambulance. I heard her telling off the agency nurse for his incompetence for several minutes. I was taken to hospital handcuffed and with two prison officers, but I did not plan on going anywhere.

I spent the next nine weeks in the prison ward of the city hospital, with prison officers who were far more friendly and caring than most at the MWCC and nurses who did not seem to care that the patients they were looking after were prisoners. One nurse took a liking to me and brought in a video every so often for me to watch. I made friends with a young man who had come from a male prison who was having an operation for testicular cancer. He joked bravely about the impending loss of his manhood and kept me company for most of the time I was on the ward.

The first few weeks I spent in the hospital I was still filled with regret and anger at myself for ruining my life, but by the time I went back to jail I had forgotten the reason I had done myself such a terrible injury and was ready to settle back into prison life once more. In the hospital I had a sketch book to draw in, a TV to watch and one of the officers even fetched a radio so I could have some music. For the first time since I had been in prison in the previous year I was a model prisoner. I did not think of hurting anyone or even myself and always did what was expected of me. When I returned to the MWCC I had a new ideal environment: the caring atmosphere of the hospital. I knew that if I was on a hospital ward I would be cared for and would not want to be violent as I was in prison. Hospital became the place that prison had seemed the year before, the place I would be happy. I did everything I could to get admitted to hospital again, not caring how much pain I caused myself and giving no thought to the scars that increased as time went on.

I no longer wanted to die but I did want to be free of the disease I seemed to have, this incurable disease of aggression that I was no longer able to control. From starting out as a defensive mechanism against violence from a fellow prisoner to improving my credibility among criminals, my violence against officers had become something apparently outside my control and seemed to have taken me over. I thought the state of aggression that plagued me was something external to myself that I could do nothing to stop. I would get a feeling somewhere between excitement and depression and I would translate that as a need to attack a screw. Coupled with this feeling was my perceived inability to survive outside of prison. I thought I was completely unable to control my violent impulses and thought that if I did not act on them they would worsen and worsen until I killed someone. Under my case manager Laura's watchful eye, I spent more and more of my time in the suicide observation cell and almost grew accustomed to my time in there. I developed a system of coping with the five days I had to spend there after being violent to an officer; I would relate the time I had been there to the time remaining so that the only days that were almost impossible to bear were the first two. After that I had already been there for half the time I had to and I 'hadn't died or anything', so it couldn't be all that bad.

I looked forward to a break from the monotony of life in the Management Unit and loved going out into the jail for any reason at all. I didn't mind that I was handcuffed and escorted by two officers or that I had to ride on the back of an electric buggy that bounced its way across the gravel paths scarily quickly for a handcuffed person who could not hold on to anything, sitting on the back of it. My favourite reason for leaving the unit was a visit from my parents or some other relative or friend of the family, but anything that got me out of Management was exciting. I even liked being interviewed by the police prisons squad, usually scary-looking detectives who I imagined were quite capable of the most extreme violence to a prisoner if provoked. They often came in to quiz me about my latest attack on an officer. A solicitor's visit was always good or a therapist or counsellor. One time I was escorted to the visits centre to meet some police officers for some unknown reason. I had done nothing worthy of the attention of the police that I could think of and wondered why detectives wanted to speak to me this time. The officers were from the major crime squad and wanted to question me about my old criminal accomplice, Joe, who had been arrested in Sydney but was pretending to be somebody else, putting on a fake Irish accent and using a false name. When I asked the police officers what he had been charged with they told me he had allegedly raped six women at knifepoint. I had no information to give the police, having not seen Joe in almost four years, but I thanked whatever gods I believed in that he had never tried to rape me.

After I had served my three months, plus another two or so for a number of attacks on prison staff, I was due to go home once more. This time I had little hope that I was not going to end up back at the MWCC but thought I should make as much of an effort as I could. I was due to move in just down the street from my girlfriend, Katie, and did not want to disappoint her any more than I already had by going back to jail. Once again my parents drove to Melbourne and picked me up at the prison gates, their van packed full of my possessions. I unpacked and left for Katie's house. When I got there I was appalled at the state of the place. There was a week's worth of dirty dishes in the sink, clothes on the floor and dirt and clutter everywhere. I was messy, but this place was squalid. I ignored the grime and mess and said hello to Katie's two dogs and two cats and thanked Katie for her getting-out gift to me, a $10 pair of tracksuit pants with buttons down the side. Katie asked me to help her with the month's worth of unpaid bills she had saved, possibly in the knowledge that I was getting out.

Katie and I spent a lot of our time over the next few weeks drinking booze of one kind or another. I invented a drink made with Kahlua, Cointreau and milk that was sickly sweet but had the desired effect of making us very drunk very quickly. We went to the casino in the inner city most nights; I would put a couple of dollars in a poker machine and be glad to win anything more than I put in, whereas Katie would spend everything she had then come and ask me for some of my money to put in her machine. One time I put in $3 and took out $100. Thinking Katie would be glad for me and want to come out drinking with my new-found wealth, I told her of my win and was asked by her for $20 so she could play her machine some more. One night I won $35 and took it home, leaving it on top of my bedside table. The next day Katie came over. When she left I noticed it had gone, along with $200 I had hidden. Katie denied stealing it and claimed someone must have broken in, but even I couldn't overlook the fact that I had been robbed by the woman who was supposed to be my lover and the closest person to me in the world. Any hope I previously had began to disappear and the despair and depression that had been with me when I was in jail came back with a vengeance. Wanting to return to jail, where at least you knew that people were going to rob you and could be on your guard, I tried a trick another girl in prison did if she wanted to go back – I rang the emergency services number and made a bomb threat on the house of State Premier Jeff Kennett (a socialist friend had given me the address some years ago and I'd remembered it). The police turned up at my door having traced the call, but instead of being taken to the MWCC again, I was sent to the psychiatric hospital. Katie accused me of everything she could think of; she could see that I was trying to escape her.

As I saw it there was no way out for me. Upon my release from the hospital I would have to return to my house and be mistreated and robbed by my girlfriend once more. A couple of days previously I had realised that my replacement bank card had not arrived in the mail and suspected that Katie had stolen it from my letter box. I still had about $1500 in the account and definitely did not want Katie to get hold of it. I searched through the mess of papers in her lounge-room, hoping she'd left it there. She came in while I was doing this and asked what I was up to, then threatened me as she thought I was going through her things. I was frightened of her, thinking that if she was capable of the things she did to hurt herself, she would probably be able to do something awful to me. I did not want to go back to jail but it seemed the only option available to me. The only other path I could take would be to go back to live with my parents, but I was terrified I might kill them during an attack of violent impulses, or that I would once again become psychotic, as I had the last time I had lived with them. I didn't want to hurt any of the nurses at the hospital, all of whom seemed very nice, but I knew how hard it was to be sent to prison if you were a committed patient in a psychiatric hospital. I picked up the knife I had used to eat my dinner with and chased a nurse, having no intention of doing anything serious to her with it but not realising that she would not know that. The poor nurse spent the next month off work on stress leave and I spent the next 21 months in prison. A week later Katie left me. She stole everything I had left at her house and moved interstate. Rather than missing her or wanting her back, I was eternally grateful to her for exiting my life and thought the loss of my possessions a small price to pay for getting away from her.

I started to see a therapist recommended to my parents by my old art teacher. The therapist's name was Alfred and he was about 45 years old. He came in twice a week and filled my head with all manner of weird theories about why I did what I did. He even gave me a 'violence doll', which I was supposed to carry with me at all times and to squeeze should I feel the need to attack anyone. He would say in his most practised therapist tone 'squeeze the doll, squeeze the doll' if he thought I was about to do anything rash. He also had what seemed to me a fascination with sexual things that I was totally unaware of and would read the most bizarre meaning into simple things. He bought me extravagant gifts, including underwear, and insisted I give him a hug every time he left. I thought he was a bit creepy but the fact that I got out of my cell to see him meant I was willing to put up with any amount of creepiness.

The medical centre once again changed hands and the prison gained a psychiatrist, an aloof and somewhat imperious man who saw the more troubled prisoners, like myself, about once a month for 15 minutes or so. I also liked to talk to this psychiatrist as it meant a break from the monotony of life in my cell.

When the medical centre changed hands we lost our psychiatric nurses and I thought my five-day punishments in the suicide observation cell must surely be a thing of the past. Unfortunately for me the latest new governor thought it an excellent idea that I pay for my crimes by being locked in the suicide observation cell for any act of violence, despite the fact that it was not intended for that. I tried as hard as I could not to give in to my impulses but it seemed an impossible task. Many officers liked me, even though I was a threat to them, and one even remarked to my mum on a visit 'Jeanette hit me yesterday, but we all love her.' But while the officers could see that perhaps I wasn't all evil, I was having a much harder time believing that I had any good in me and thought I deserved all the awful things that I'd obviously brought upon myself through my wrongdoing.

A lot of my fellow prisoners were dying from drug overdoses on their release and I was reminded of my own mortality. Seven women I had known in prison died within a two-month period and I got very scared. I believed that God must be punishing me for turning away from him in my youth and started asking the officers to let me go to the chapel as often as I could. I liked talking to the chaplain, Beth. She was a great listener and would hold my hands and say a prayer for me. I even started taking communion, although I wasn't 100 per cent convinced that was going to help at all. I prayed to God to rid me of my affliction of liking being in prison and attacking prison officers. I prayed to get out and I prayed for forgiveness for all the apparently terrible things I'd done that I felt no remorse for. I prayed to be able to feel something for all the prison officers and psychiatric nurses I had hit or threatened over the last three years. I took to praying in my head most of the day, hoping it would make some difference to how I felt. God was once again going to be my best friend.

The toughest girl in the prison was undoubtedly Clare. The second-most fearsome was her cousin, Gayle. They had both been in the Management Unit as long as I had, but unlike me they had inflicted some serious physical damage on their victim, a young girl who had informed on one of Clare's friends and who they'd stabbed with a broken piece of glass in another unit of the prison, almost killing her. I had always got along with both these frightening characters through my usual survival mechanism – my ability to play whatever role was expected of me and to do everything within my power to please. One day though, about six weeks before I was due to be released, I had an argument with Clare and a friend of hers. I yelled at the both of them from the other side of the unit, separated by a bullet-proof glass screen. The officers knew if they let me back into the unit with Clare and her cousin my life would be very nasty indeed, so I was left on the other side of the unit by myself. A couple of days later the prison authorities moved a group of Protection prisoners into the same side of the unit as me. I thought that at last I would have someone to talk to and had stopped caring that these women were informers and worse. I wanted some company and I was getting out in six weeks, so who cared if I got a reputation for talking to 'dogs' (informers). I asked the officer on duty if I could be let out of my cell to mix with the new arrivals but he told me that under no circumstances would I be allowed out. I was desperate and pleaded with everyone I could find, even the commissioner for corrections who was conducting a routine inspection of the prison. She too said 'no' and I had nowhere left to turn.

For the last six weeks of my sentence I spent half an hour per day out of my cell and had no contact with another living soul, with the exception of the screw in charge of the unit who wanted nothing to do with me. The main thing I had liked about being in prison was the fact that I was never lonely, yet now I was so lonely I thought I might die. I prayed constantly, every hour I was awake, for God to let me mix with anyone, for me to have a friend, yet apparently my prayer was not answered. The only people with whom I had a conversation in that six weeks were my parents who came for a two-hour visit, a social worker and my rather creepy therapist who promised some kind of justice for me and said he would see me twice a week when I got out. I no longer wanted to die and I now knew I no longer wanted to return to prison as long as I lived. An officer made a bet that if I stayed out for a month he'd give me ten packets of cigarettes. I happily shook on it, knowing that this time I was never coming back.

9.

Educating the Mad

A social worker had been visiting me while I was still in prison, assessing my suitability to attend a psychiatric rehabilitation programme when I got out. The programme was called 'Rainbow' and was for women with a diagnosis of borderline personality disorder, something I had been told I had by the prison psychiatrist and my therapist. This disorder usually affects people who have had some major trauma in childhood or later in life, and causes people to do destructive and negative things such as harming themselves or engaging in dangerous behaviour. When I had been told that this was my problem I had breathed a big sigh of relief, glad that the professionals seemed to think I did not have Asperger Syndrome. Rainbow had been set up only a year before I was released and was in its very early stages. The staff there were worried I would pose a threat to their clients or staff and sent the social worker, Tania, to visit me in prison several times to gauge whether or not I would benefit from the programme and would be able to stay out of trouble. Eventually it was decided that I would be accepted into the Rainbow programme on release, news that cheered me up a bit and gave me some much needed hope.

The night before I was released was the hottest of the summer and I was unable to sleep because of both the heat and the excitement and nervousness I felt at the prospect of being in the outside world again after nearly two years. I packed the few possessions in my cell and waved goodbye to the MWCC for what I hoped with all my heart would be the last time. My parents were once again waiting for me at the gate and they drove me to my new home. One of the staff at Rainbow greeted me and explained all the rules, what I could and could not do, consequences for me should I misbehave and so on. He then led me to the one-bedroom flat I would be staying in. I met a nurse who said she would be available to me at any time should I need some company or someone to talk things over with. I was to have a nurse to talk to all day, every day for the entire time I was in this unit.

I soon settled in, loving the constant possibility of someone to talk to me after six weeks of almost complete isolation. I was quite fragile though, and had to write myself lists of reasons why I did not want to return to jail. I loved the material side of being 'on the outside' and, as my rent was only $45 per week, I had lots of money left over to spend on nice things. The first thing I needed was a stereo so I could play relaxing music when I went to sleep. I then started buying CDs and tapes, usually getting a new one each week. But the best material thing I had on the outside that was unavailable in prison was the coffee. I'd always been a bit of a coffee snob, only liking the high-quality, perco-lator-type coffee and all they had in jail was the cheapest, most revolting brand of instant coffee there was. As a free woman I marvelled at the choice of delicious ground coffee available and savoured every mouthful of each new cup.

The nurses were all wonderfully caring and great to talk to. It seemed that their purpose was to entertain me. I did sometimes feel a strong urge to hit them, but my life was fast becoming enjoyable and I did not want to return to jail. One of the social workers who ran the group therapy programme had told me that urges to hurt oneself or others *passed* if you let them and that each time you resisted they were less likely to bother you. This was news to me, wonderful news. What's more, it was actually true! If I felt violent or wanted to hurt myself and I gave in to it, it would return, yet the more I refused to give in to my impulses, the less they bothered me. I wondered why no one in the prison had informed me of this useful fact, thinking it would have made my life a lot easier had I known this. As the days went on I wanted to hurt people less and less frequently and the effort of not giving in to my impulses and the success I was having, coupled with the support and encouragement of the Rainbow staff, was giving me something I had not experienced in years – a sense of pride in myself.

I actually enjoyed spending time with my nurses. We would go swimming or drive into the countryside, finding ourselves in some pretty little town or marvelling at the tall trees. I had bought my dad's old camera that he'd had since the 1980s and started taking photos of things I thought were beautiful. I had some links to my old life though, and rang the prison most nights to speak to my favourite officer, a gentle, thoughtful woman named Dale who had always had faith in me, even when I had none in myself. I had made a conscious break with the more negative aspects of my old life and had thrown out the phone number of a dope dealer a fellow prisoner had given me months ago and I had held onto all that time. I did not intend to smoke drugs again, finally understanding the effects marijuana had on my mental health and thinking that smoking dope would send me into a psychotic state again. I was working hard at all the little tasks and worksheets the staff from the group therapy programme and nurses had set me and I was determined to convince all concerned that I had the resolve to enter the programme with the women I had met who were doing it. Six weeks after I left prison my case worker told me I was to move into the shared house where the women in the group programme lived and the next day start the therapy programme. I felt more pride and happiness than I had for years.

I did not have a lot of things to move into my new house with, Katie having stolen almost everything I had owned during my last time in prison. I had bought a number of nice things with which to decorate my room and my parents had luckily been holding onto my books and things from my childhood, but I had few clothes save those I had bought recently with the money I had been given by the prison authorities on leaving. I owned no furniture or kitchen utensils and most of what I owned consisted of letters from my time in prison and

CDs and videos I had bought in the last few weeks while living in my one-bedroom unit rented through Rainbow.

I felt ashamed of my recent past when speaking to my new housemates, although I felt I had to tell them I had been in prison. They all seemed to have friends and family who rang them all the time and cared, and, while I was in contact with my parents almost every day, they were the only people that I knew well enough to call. I lived in fear of running into anyone I had known whilst in jail as I felt I needed to make a complete break with my past. The only exception to this rule was my friendship with 'Mad-Bomber Jones' – a young woman who, like me, had come from a middle-class background, but could not stop making bomb threats so she could end up in prison. While the shortest period of time I had spent out of custody in the time I was going to prison was one week, Mad-Bomber's record was three hours. She had been released a few weeks before me and was trying her hardest to stay out of trouble. She lived in an inner suburb of Melbourne a long way from where I was staying but I went to visit her a few times. Each time I visited Mad-Bomber I was struck by how interested she was in the goings on at the women's prison. She kept newspaper clippings about the place and recorded every item about the MWCC on the TV news onto a special video tape. She was trying to get her driver's licence but I suspected that once she achieved that goal she would return to where she felt most at home, prison.

On the way home from my first visit with Mad-Bomber I bumped into a woman I had known in prison, Angie. Angie was from Vietnam and spoke Mandarin. We had conversed together in Mandarin in prison as her English was not good. In prison I had enjoyed her company, but now I was out I wanted nothing to do with anyone who reminded me of what I thought of as my terrible past. When I saw her on the outside I did not recognise her as she had lost a lot of weight from using heroin every day. She asked me in Chinese if I had any money and I left her with a $20 note and gave her my phone number at Rainbow for when she wanted to pay me back. When I returned she had already called and I panicked. There was a real live heroin addict I had been in jail with wanting to be my friend and I didn't know what to do. I told the other residents at the house to vet the phone calls and tell Angie she'd dialled the wrong number if she called again. I didn't care about the $20 that I knew I would never see again and was relieved that I didn't have to face up to the previous life I was trying so hard to escape.

The group therapy programme consisted of meditation every morning followed by 'skills training' in which we learned ways of dealing with the problems people with borderline personality disorder experience. I was struck by how much harder than me everyone else seemed to be finding the course; how the skills sessions brought out repressed memories and past experiences they would rather forget and how the course challenged most people's rather set ideas. I did not experience any problems like this. In fact the only problems I really had were those of controlling my impulses to hurt myself. After a couple of months at Rainbow I rarely had any violent impulses towards others and considered myself cured of this problem. The only other problem I had was that of being in close contact with a group of depressed and traumatised people who seemed to work on so many levels I could not keep up. I liked my fellow residents and through knowing them developed some kind of understanding of the experiences of others, but living in close contact with such a troubled group of women made it almost impossible for me to ever separate their problems from my mind. I was always worrying that someone would kill themselves or try some psychological game I didn't understand and involve me in their problems. While I lived at the shared house at Rainbow I was never relaxed.

While I didn't enjoy living in close proximity to so many troubled people, I didn't have much choice in the matter and, on top of that, I had developed a phobia of being alone. I thought I could not be alone without some unknown but terrible thing happening and had trouble even spending an hour in my own company. I was nevertheless determined to overcome any of the problems that made my life unpleasant and practised being by myself for longer and longer periods. The Rainbow staff were always supportive and ready to listen to whatever problem myself or another resident may have and I spent many hours in the company of one or other of the staff discussing some issue or another I could not mention in group therapy.

I was struck by how much I differed from the other women in the programme, although I never questioned my diagnosis of borderline personality disorder. Other residents had huge attachment issues and were terrified of the day their six-month stay would be over and they would no longer see the staff every day. I had never formed a strong attachment with anyone and didn't even grieve when family members had died, so the idea of leaving the Rainbow staff behind caused me very little anxiety. While my logical side could accept the predicament of the other women, I had no idea of the emotions involved in attachment to another. Most other women relived traumatic experiences, but I had the emotional memory of a bag of sugar and only occasionally recalled what feeling sad or frightened was like. I would sometimes have some nameless surge of emotional discomfort when confronted with something that triggered a memory but as to having 'flashbacks' of negative experiences or being able to relive a moment from the past, I had no idea. In fact the only two things I seemed to have in common with my housemates was the fact that I had a problem controlling impulses to hurt myself and the fact that I didn't like myself. The staff continually congratulated me on my progress and hard work but to me the other residents were all working twice as hard as me and actually had major problems. As I saw it I had made the decision not to return to prison and done a bit of work controlling my impulses but apart from that I'd just said what I thought was expected of me in group therapy and skills training, and said the kinds of words of comfort I thought the other women wanted to hear when they were upset. Once again I was acting but it seemed the only person aware of it was me.

After three months in the group programme, I moved into my own little flat. Still rented out by Rainbow, it was a two-bedroom unit a short walk from the building where therapy sessions were held. The main difference between my new home and my old one was that now I was living alone, a huge step for someone who only months ago was afraid to spend two or three hours in their own company. I took to living alone almost immediately and grew very attached to my stereo and the two rocking chairs in the lounge-room on which I would rock for hours at a time. This was the most exhilarating feeling, especially with the music blaring in the background. I knew that if someone moved in with me my world would once again be filled with the problems and insecurities of others and that I would lose my favourite things: my own company and the freedom to do whatever took my fancy. I was having a lot of trouble sleeping and usually awoke at 1 or 2 in the morning, staying up the rest of the night and stumbling, half asleep, to the programme at 8.30 am It was only during these early mornings that I became lonely or depressed, but I didn't mind because I knew that the next day I would be able to talk to the staff at the programme and the other residents. I always arrived for the day's sessions with a smile on my face and a conversation at the ready.

I decided, towards the end of my six-month stay at Rainbow, that I would apply for entry to an art course, maybe at one of the three universities in Melbourne that offered a degree in Fine Arts. I was feeling hopeful and optimistic and thought a university course would be an excellent way to structure my time and a degree would give me some pride in myself. I set about gathering the relevant forms and sent off my application, knowing I would not hear back for a few months but feeling excited at the prospect of study anyway. I was treated like the star of the programme and the staff would discuss my ability to recite all of the skills sessions in the order they came in the course, even knowing which page they were on in the big black folder the staff had presented me with on entry to the programme. I knew I would miss all the company I had at Rainbow and wrote down the phone numbers of all the residents, thinking it would be a lot nicer to see them socially than in a therapy programme and that I needed to have some friends or I would be very lonely when I moved out.

I had found a place to stay and, while it was very cheap, it depressed me to think about living there and I was looking around for somewhere else from the first day I paid my rent. The room I rented was in a boarding house in the inner suburbs, a place for women to stay when they had nowhere else to go. I started staying there on the weekends while I was still at Rainbow so as to get used to living there.

The room was tiny and the other residents were mostly women who had just been discharged from psychiatric hospital. Every weekend I stayed in this house I was depressed and could not imagine living there permanently, but I had no other options. Luckily I was still in contact with the outreach social worker employed by Rainbow, Tania, and she was very knowledgeable about practical things like accommodation. She told me of a house run by a community mental health organisation where 10–12 people could live at once, Edna Hurley House. I thought all this free company sounded wonderful and was pleased when Tania told me most of the residents there were quite 'well' and not just out of hospital. I went to an interview and knew that this was where I wanted to live. The house was spacious, the people were not my worst idea of 'crazy people' and seemed quite friendly and there was public transport right near the front door, a tram that went through leafy, affluent suburbs. I would have to wait to find out if my interview was successful. In the meantime, I finally left Rainbow and was driven by my parents in their van to the boarding house I had been staying at at the weekends. I spent the whole time I lived in that house dreaming of moving to Edna Hurley House and didn't mind so much that my current housemates were either severely psychotic or just plain annoying. I sat in my room, watching my tiny second-hand television, not even caring when a huge spider wandered in one night or when the heroin addict in the next room almost burned the house down, smoking in bed. I had one friend, a woman I had met at Rainbow, Amanda, and I called her every night, thinking how sweet she must be to put up with my constant phone calls. I had my parents who were always willing to listen to my complaints about the crazy fundamentalist Christian lady who stuck home-made 'Jesus loves you' cards under everyone's door or the prostitute whose customers kept me awake most nights banging around the house with no respect for its other occupants. I tried hard to be positive and look forward to a future in which I had the possibility of going to art school once more and moving into Edna Hurley House.

While living at the boarding house I had a habit of reading meaning into events that were completely unrelated to my life. When the Sydney Olympic games were on TV I anxiously watched as Australian athlete Cathy Freeman competed in her 400-metre race and thought that if she won the gold medal my life would somehow become instantly perfect and all my dreams would be fulfilled. She did win and, as Australians celebrated victory for their country, I celebrated the victory I thought 'our Cathy' had won for my future. I would see trams going down the street and predict future events in my life based on how many I saw while I was out. I was so happy when the three trams I saw in five minutes one day signalled, in my mind, that I was going to be accepted to Edna Hurley House. My anxiety about life either lessened or increased depending on whether I thought the events of the day had signified good or bad outcomes for my aspirations.

My interpretation of the magical goings on of the world seemed to have been correct as, after having lived in the boarding house for two months, I had a phone call from one of the staff at Edna Hurley House to tell me I had been accepted. My social worker, Tania, offered to help me move and before long I had left my unstable and drug-addicted housemates behind and was living in the place I had fantasised about for the past two months.

Edna Hurley House was situated in a fairly well-off suburb, full of tree-lined streets and expensive shops. The residents of the house were some of the few poorer inhabitants of the suburb and looked a little out of place in the expensive cafes and gift shops that were dotted everywhere in sight. The house had 12 occupants including myself when I moved in, as many as could live there at one time. I soon got to know them all. A pretty girl, a little younger than me, Anne, looked like a good person to be a new friend and I soon spent my days with her and two other girls at the house about her age. We all got along well and they didn't seem to mind that I had something of a dubious past. I was not sure whether or not to tell people I had been in prison when I moved in, but my sense of honesty meant that I couldn't stop myself from saying where I had spent three years of my life in the last few years. I thought that if I said I had been out of prison for less than a year, everyone would be much more scared of me than if I got a bit creative with the truth and told them my time in prison had been a little longer ago. I had to invent a year of my life to fit in with my lie and put a lot of energy into keeping people convinced. As I had been on the other occasions I hadn't been honest, I was surprised as to how ready people were to believe my lies. I wanted with every inch of my being to tell the truth but I was too scared of my fellow residents judging me and not accepting me for knowing I had been involved in violent criminal activity so recently.

There were four staff members at the house, two social workers, a psychologist and a woman with a background in art therapy. They were there from 9 am to 5 pm on weekdays. When they were around we had meetings and activities and when they were away we did whatever we wanted. There was a policy at the house that no one was allowed to drink alcohol inside, but when the staff were not there most residents would sneak in beer or wine from time to time. While at Rainbow I had rarely touched anything stronger than coffee, having been told by the staff there that alcohol was not good for mental health. I had taken to rigidly following any of the 'rules' given to me by the people I saw as 'the authorities' and was terrified of breaking any of them, thinking that some minor wrongdoing on my part would lead me on a path to prison. However, when I got to Edna Hurley House I relaxed my social piety somewhat. Seeing that the residents I respected and had become my new friends all drank, I thought it couldn't hurt to have a beer every so often and even felt a naughty thrill at sneaking in bottles when the staff weren't looking. I was soon drinking heavily at least once a week and had discovered 'the hang-over' for the first time in my life. I would not touch marijuana though, knowing that if I smoked that drug regularly I would probably become psychotic once more and may even go back to prison. Even if I was in a resident's room and everyone was puffing on a joint I wouldn't consider taking even one drag. While I did enjoy far too many beers on occasion, I never again intended to touch drugs.

When I had settled into life at Edna Hurley House I received letters from the three art schools I had applied to months before. I had inter-views for two drawing and three painting courses. I spent many hours sorting through my large collection of artworks, some executed eight years previously, and faced the hard decision of what to include. I did the best job I could of narrowing my huge collection down to a good selection of works and set off for my interviews. The interviews ranged from the apparently successful ones where the interviewers were friendly and seemed genuinely interested in my work, to the obviously unsuccessful, including one at my old school, RMIT, where one lecturer lined up my photographs of old paintings and asked me why I thought they 'didn't work'. I was told I would know the results within a few weeks and went home trying to think positive thoughts about how I had gone, while not getting my hopes up too much. I expected to be allowed back to RMIT considering I had studied there before, but got a letter from both the drawing and painting departments from that school informing me I had been unsuccessful. The Victorian College of the Arts also did not offer me a place. I was now just waiting for my letter from Monash, the school that was the furthest away from the city and whose course had seemed the hardest. When the letter arrived I feared to open it, much as I had with my letter from RMIT eight years before. With shaking hands I opened the envelope and let out a triumphant yell. I had been accepted.

I was quite nervous at the prospect of returning to study and knew I would find myself inventing the past few years of my life when talking to the other students, so as to avoid them finding out I'd been in prison. I went to Monash on student orientation day and found the place quite daunting. I was lost frequently and did not know anyone. I started to try to talk to some new students but was nervous and didn't know what to say. Trying to make conversation, I commented to an approachable-looking older woman that it was good that not everyone was young and gorgeous. I was paranoid, seeing things in my mind that weren't there. I went to the toilet and was convinced there were cameras watching me and sending the pictures to a group of laughing gorgeous people. I did the best I could to pull myself together and tried hard not to be intimidated by my fellow students.

A week later lectures started and I met the rest of my class. I didn't talk to anyone for a few weeks and was terrified of everyone, especially of people finding out about 'my past'. I had overcome the feelings of inadequacy about my abilities as an artist that had plagued me throughout my time at RMIT though, and realised that all the students in my first-year class had similar abilities at painting and that there really wasn't all that much difference between us. I was not the 'worst' or the 'best', I was simply another student with little experience of painting who wanted to improve their skills. Amazingly, other students seemed to think *I* was the star student, one woman even asking me if I was a genius. I started trying to play the role of a student once more and hid almost everything about my life outside of art school from my fellow students. No one at Monash knew that I lived in a house with 11 other people, all of whom had a mental illness. Nobody knew I had been in prison. I confined my discussion with people at school to topics about art and art only, hoping that my secrets would be safe. While I was very reticent to talk to other students for fear they would discover my secret past, I started looking forward to going to Monash to paint and draw and learn about art history. I hardly missed a class and dedicated most of my spare time to working on projects for art school. I was also surprised to discover that my old friend from my RMIT days, Lee, was now teaching at Monash. I didn't recognise him when I saw him for the first time in five years, but after a bit we started talking and catching up on news. Apart from my family, he was the only person in my life who had known me before I had been in prison. Lee never once judged me or criticised me and that gave me a huge amount of respect for him.

The week before the mid-year break from university I was given a kitten. Her owner was the brother of one of the women at Edna Hurley House who was moving overseas and could not look after his little cat. I had been wanting a cat since my release from prison and had felt part of me was missing in the absence of a pet. Tilly came to my house in a box, scared and yowling. I fed her and patted her for ages. I was so happy and I now had a companion who would come with me every-where I went. Tilly befriended all my fellow residents at Edna Hurley House and I quickly fell in love with her unique nature and quirky ways. I missed three days of university to be with my new friend, the only days I'd missed all semester, and for once I didn't care if I got a bit behind in my work. Once again I had a feline friend.

While I rarely felt any negative, threatening emotions and was not depressed, I was very sensitive and emotional if I was stressed or anxious. I was beginning to develop a hatred of my drawing class for its effects on my mental state. This class lasted five hours and finished at 7 pm, when it was dark outside. It involved a large amount of concentration and I always tried my hardest to make a good drawing. By the end of this endurance session I would be frazzled, tired and stressed and started experiencing things I could well have lived without. On the walk to the train station after this class I would get paranoid thoughts that strangers were talking about me and laughing at me. I would feel an impulse to attack them, similar to the feelings I felt in prison. I dreaded the drawing class and hoped and prayed each time I went to it that I would escape feeling aggressive and paranoid afterwards. I also started thinking that I needed a paid job, and, as I was apparently doing so well as a student, thought I would have no trouble working either. Whenever I thought about working I would be seized by panic and would think I was bound to be terrible at anything I did but I eventually got a job washing dishes in a restaurant where one of the women who lived in my house worked. I was obsessed with my work and spent most of the time anticipating my one shift each week and worrying that I would do something 'bad' that would cost me my job. I was stressed all the time and no amount of cups of tea, baths or television seemed to be able to relax me.

After I had worked my one shift a week for five weeks I became so paranoid and stressed that I went totally mad. I thought I was going to jail and that people were trying to kill me. I felt an urge to be violent all the time and was so scared I was going to attack someone that I avoided going out. I ended up spending some time in psychiatric hospital again, this time only for a few days. I did not go to university during the final three weeks of the school year and thought I surely must have failed the year, this only making me feel worse. I filled out the forms for a 'special consideration' and waited for my results, being too depressed and paranoid to really care what they were. After a couple of weeks I had a phone call from my drawing lecturer. Puzzled, I asked why she had called and she informed me that I had topped the year in drawing and had won a prize. I was baffled – after all I had missed more than half the drawing classes and thought my work in the ones I did attend was shoddy at best. The lecturer said I would have to go to the opening of the graduating students' exhibition to accept my prize. Rather than being happy about this I was apprehensive; I knew that going to a crowded opening would mean I felt an urge to attack people. I nevertheless forced myself to go to the opening and received my prize.

For the next three months I was plagued by the urge to attack people. Through sheer determination I managed to hold back from doing anything to anyone and the feelings gradually got easier to deal with. I still didn't like going out in public, but it was bearable. I had gained a lot of confidence in my ability to handle such problems and was pretty sure I would never return to prison. I started my second year of university feeling a little fragile, but trusting in my ability to cope.

Second years had a bigger studio to work in and we all got our own little spot. My studio space was between a mature-age student, Jasmine, and a young man, Tom. I started to get to know people in my year a lot better now that I had a studio to call my own – I did not feel so overwhelmed by the people and mess everywhere and the fact that no one was in the same place from one day to the next. I even told two people that I had been in prison, although I played it down as much as I could. I lived in constant dread of the whole class knowing my secret and begged the two people I'd told to keep it to themselves. In first year we had been set projects to do but now we were left to our own devices with the lecturers commenting on the self-directed artwork we made. I knew what I wanted to make art about – my past – but I was much too scared to do so. As I saw it my past was still very recent and I had no intention of inviting the judgement of my whole class. I spent my second year painting pretty little images of buildings, paintings that none of my lecturers found very impressive. My fellow students tended to think more highly of my paintings than my teachers and some were outraged on my behalf when I received quite a low mark for my painting subject. One student was so taken with my work he asked me if I would exhibit with him at a gallery near where I lived. Excited about the prospect of my first art show since 1996, I happily accepted and set about planning the works I would show in the gallery later that year. The advent of an exhibition brought with it stressful associations with my past and my excitement soon turned to nerves as I related my last experience of exhibiting to my present situation; I was terrified that for some reason history would repeat itself and I would go to prison three days into the exhibition. I tried my hardest to relax. Thankfully, the show was not for a few months and I did eventually stop worrying about it and concentrated on my studies and on spending time with my new girlfriend, Helen.

Helen was a fellow resident at Edna Hurley House and was about the same age as me. We made friends almost as soon as she moved in, having a love of academic study, philosophy and art in common. After I had known Helen for about six months she asked me if I wanted to go out with her and, without thinking twice, I agreed. It was co-dependence at first sight. I was desperate for a companion, as I had been in the past, and did not stop to consider the implications of going out with someone like Helen; someone with a lot of insecurities and with needs that I was incapable of meeting. Helen was sweet and kind and thoughtful. She would surprise me with wonderful gifts and give me little cards with poems she'd written on them, poems written especially for me. At first I thought nothing could ever go wrong with our relationship, but before long I found myself wanting more time away from Helen and felt that maybe I should have put some thought into my decision to go out with her. Helen had many psychological problems and seemed to be unable to do anything about them herself. She relied on others to cheer her up and offer her hope and, when I was just friends with her, I found this quite easy. Yet as soon as we started going out I found it harder and harder to make anything better for her. I could not do what was expected of me and felt increasingly hopeless. I was also getting annoyed with things she said and did that, if anyone other than Helen had said or done them, would not have bothered me in the least bit. I had to pretend that I was not on the verge of slapping my girlfriend or yelling at her, feeling that I was being petty. After all, I thought, she didn't deserve my anger and pointing out how I was feeling probably wouldn't help matters.

As the months went by, I started thinking that it was Helen, not I, that was getting all the attention and that I was the poor sucker doing all the giving. I could not see any advantage in our staying together but feared that, in her unstable state, Helen might do something harmful to herself should I leave her. I spent about two months pretending not to be angry and dreaming of being single again. I could see a light ahead as my exhibition approached. I was planning to move out of Edna Hurley House to a flat on my own after my show and Helen did not want to travel the distance to visit me, preferring instead that I should visit her. I hoped that maybe seeing each other less often might make me feel a bit better about the situation.

Two days after I moved out, Helen took an overdose of her psychiatric medication and went to hospital. When she was discharged she went to stay at her parents' house and I thought she had ample support to deal with me leaving her. I'd had enough of worrying about what she may do, of feeling I hadn't been given anything emotionally except more things to worry about and most of all of trying to control my constant anger when in her company. There was no way I could give Helen what she needed or that she could give me what I wanted. I called her to tell her it was over and breathed an enormous sigh of relief at my new freedom as a single woman. I decided then to give some thought to any proposition of a relationship in the future, rather than saying, as I had to Helen when she asked me, 'Yeah, why not?'

10.

Forgetting the Script

Just before I moved into my new flat, I accepted something about myself that had been threatening and challenging me for years – I now believed, for the first time in my life, that what I had been told in 1994 while a prisoner at Fairlea was indeed the case; I had Asperger Syndrome. I did not mind as much that I was 'different', that I moved in another world to most people. I started attending an employment service for people with autism and related conditions and felt more comfortable with myself for knowing there was a reason for the many difficult things I had experienced in my past. I was still quite embarrassed by my difference and would keep the fact of my Asperger Syndrome to myself, so as to avoid having to 'confess' to those I knew. I thought it a far more guilty secret than the fact that I had spent more than three years of my life in prison, a fact that I was finding a lot easier to tell people. I admitted to myself that I had Asperger Syndrome but that didn't mean I had to tell anyone else.

I started having long conversations with my mum, discussing the things I found almost impossible that others took for granted, like understanding the meaning of facial expressions or knowing whether someone was joking or not. While still uncomfortable with the fact that I was a member of an apparently strange minority, I could at least accept it to myself. I knew why I liked being alone, why I'd had universally bad experiences in relationships and why I was incapable of truly knowing how my actions impacted on others. I had worked out my own practically foolproof method of knowing right from wrong; a system entirely based on rationality and logic, my own personal system of empathy and ethics. I related things people might do to me and, if I didn't like the idea of someone doing it to me, I knew it was wrong to do it. I imagined that if somebody punched me in the face it would hurt and frighten me so therefore I should not punch anyone in the face. My system was a little harder with more abstract things than physical aggression or theft, but the principle was pretty much the same. I had gained a reputation among some of my friends for being 'wise', something I found incredibly hard to accept but which seemed to stick. I had never considered myself wise but I did seem to always know the right thing to say and do even if there was no feeling behind it other than 'What would be the most sensible thing to say in this situation?' My many experiences of the darker side of the world had taught me a lot about the things that motivated others.

I had been granted a two-bedroom flat to stay in whilst on the waiting list for public housing, a huge flat all to myself in an affluent suburb. It had a bright green carpet, which I loved, and came with furniture and a $350 grant to spend on anything I wanted, providing it was not a TV. I cherished the freedom I had in my own place, with no one but my cat Tilly to bother me or leave their dishes in the sink. I had started speaking to my brother, Dean, again. He had become as much of a friend as anyone I knew. He and his girlfriend Carolyn lived in the next suburb and I often spent time with them and enjoyed having them close by. I invited them to a low-key party at my flat, which was only attended by five people but enjoyed by all.

My flat was a 25-minute walk away from university, so I could get up late and still make it to class with time to spare. On the first day of my final year I greeted my fellow third years and started painting immediately. I intended to paint more pretty pictures of houses but what came out, for some reason, was an abstract painting with score-marks, like the marks prisoners in old movies scratch on their cell walls to mark the passage of time. Feeling very exposed and somewhat guilty I made a series of small paintings dealing with ideas arising from my past, although in such an abstract way that only myself and my teacher, Lee, who knew more about my past than any of my colleagues, would have known what I was painting about.

As the weeks went on I grew braver and soon gained a reputation as someone who dealt with the darker things in life. I even plucked up the courage to tell some fellow students about some of the things I had experienced in my past. I could now talk more freely to people and I made some friends from among my fellow third years. I had also started to move away from just painting and was trying my hand at installations, drawings, sculpture and photography. Now I did not feel unworthy to talk to the art students who were trying more experimental forms of art; rather, I wanted to be one of them.

I fantasised about buying a video camera. I wanted to make arty films, but I had nowhere near the amount of money I needed to pay for a camera. I called my dad and asked him if he would be willing to loan me $1000 and to my utter amazement he said 'yes'. I researched the various cameras on the market and found a good quality camera that was on special offer for $999. When I brought it home I was almost too excited to open the box in case I broke it before I'd even tried to use it. I busied myself with the instruction book and learned what to do and what not to do to look after my camera. I played at making videos and tried all the functions and special features. I devised many projects that would work well on film and tried to realise them as best I could.

Initially I developed a bit of a mental block with editing my films on the school's computers and was terrified the other students in the computer lab would somehow *know* that I had no idea of what I was doing and laugh at me. After many fruitless attempts at editing through my VCR and television set I bit the bullet and had a go on the school's computers, using the easiest editing program they had. I found editing was not as hard as I'd thought and was surprised when teachers and students alike told me I was 'good with computers'. I'd never thought of myself as someone who was up with technology and had only known how to send e-mails for a couple of years, but the combined opinion of almost everyone who knew me was that I had a good head for computers. By the time assessment came around I had made a 20-minute video artwork that all the lecturers agreed was the best work I'd done in my whole time at Monash. I was as excited as I'd ever been before about this praise and started to really believe I could be a professional artist.

My grandma in England turned 100 and the entire family had a huge party to celebrate her 'century'. My parents, Dean and I were all unable to attend the party but my mum and dad decided it would be nice for Grandma to see us before she died. I still owed my parents for the video camera, so I thought I would be unable to afford the airfare. My parents discussed it and it was decided that I would go with my dad and my parents would pay for my ticket. I looked forward to seeing my English relatives, even though the last time I had gone I had been thoroughly miserable and had spent most of the time wanting to come home. This time I wasn't a criminal, a drug addict or a socialist and had even been known to go to church on occasion. I was sure my aunts would now accept me for who I was but I was nervous about the journey to England. For some reason I had become terrified of air travel and thought the plane might crash on the way. I even had nightmares about planes flying over war-zones and colliding with other planes. I told myself it was just a phobia and tried to comfort myself by thinking that driving in a car was more likely to result in death than boarding a plane.

My cat Tilly was sent to stay with Dean and Carolyn, the post office was asked to hold my mail and my one friendly neighbour offered to clean out the junk-mail from my letter box, so a potential thief would think I was still at home. I packed my clothes, a sketchbook, some reading material and my favourite thing, my beautiful video camera, and headed off to the airport. I was nervous going through customs and waiting in the departure lounge, a fact not helped at all by the electrical fire in the terminal that left all the passengers standing on the tarmac for an hour, but when the plane finally got up in the air I calmed down.

After the hellish journey I had come to expect, we arrived in London on a rainy summer's day. It was 4 am but daylight, and everyone seemed a bit rude and rushed. I thought the woman at the money change bureau at Heathrow airport had a problem with Australians, but my dad told me that people in big cities were often rushed and 'short' with strangers. I was thrilled to be in England and wanted to go everywhere there was to go. I was struck by ideas of difference and that, just by me saying something, people knew I was not from the same place as them. I now felt confident as myself, even if a little embarrassed by the knowledge that I sounded different from everyone when I spoke.

We drove in our rented car to Torquay, on the south-west coast of England. I was very apprehensive about seeing my aunt Jean, the aunt who had called me 'wicked' at that dinner in the other life that was my past. I hoped she did not still judge me by the troubled person I was. I needn't have feared though, for as soon as we arrived aunt Jean welcomed me and my dad and poured us each a large gin and tonic. After an evening at her and my uncle Dave's house I knew I had found a friend in my aunt and strangely she now reminded me of myself in some ways.

We visited my grandma on most of the days we were in England. Grandma had lived in a retirement home run by the Christadelphians for a few years and when we arrived the staff at the home greeted us warmly, telling us they had heard nothing from 'Mrs Purkis' but news of our visit. The first day we went to see her, Grandma was excited to see my dad but asked me who I was, thinking I was a man due to a combination of my short hair and her failing eyesight. Every day we saw her she made some comment about me 'looking like a man' or that it would be 'nice' if I wore a 'pretty dress'. I regretted my decision not to include some feminine clothes when packing, but found the situation amusing. Aunt Jean and my dad found the whole thing more offensive than I did and, while I was pleased that they were sticking up for my right to look how I pleased, I really didn't mind my grandma's comments and thought that, at her age, she could be forgiven for being set in her ways.

The day before we left for Australia we visited Grandma for what we all knew would be the last time. It was a sad occasion and none of us wanted that final 'goodbye' to arrive. Our visit lasted longer than on any of the previous days as both my dad and me wanted to put off the moment we would have to leave. When we eventually walked out the door, my grandma smiled at me and said 'You're a good girl, Jeanette', to which I replied 'And you're a wonderful grandma.' I felt so grateful to her for showing she had faith in me and believed me to be 'good', I wanted to stay longer in England and spend more time with my grandmother, this woman who had been my favourite person when I was a little girl and who had written me frequent letters when I was in prison when I was older.

When I got home and collected my mail from the post office, I found a letter from the Office of Housing. There was a public housing flat for me to move into. While my rent would be next to nothing I was not 100 per cent sure what my neighbours would be like, especially if I had to move into a high-rise block. The area I was moving to was in a working-class suburb of Melbourne near where I had moved when I first left home. My flat was in a huge block of other Housing Commission flats, but, to my relief, not in a high-rise tower.

The phone had not been connected in my new flat. I had to call the company and complain from a pay phone in the middle of the block of flats. There were lots of people that I thought looked 'scary' hanging around and there seemed to be an awful lot of cheeky little kids. When the phone finally was connected I checked my messages and found four missed calls from Dean. When I called him back, he excitedly told me that he had proposed to his girlfriend, Carolyn, and she had accepted! I was happy for both of them and secretly hoped they might soon produce a niece or nephew for me to play with. The wedding was set for January and I was asked to make a video of the occasion.

The first day I lived in my new flat I had to miss a class at Monash and wait for a repairman to come and fix the stove, which was not connected to the gas yet. I sat inside, feeling scared and wondering what my neighbours would do if they knew I had a computer and a video camera. I saw some guys who looked like they did drugs and my nervousness grew. I didn't want any trouble from druggies and did not even complain when a football was accidentally kicked into my window several times by some likely-looking lads. On my second day in my new home I heard a knock on the door and nervously answered it. There was a young woman in a Muslim scarf smiling at me. I let her in and made a pot of tea. She introduced herself as Carly and invited me to meet some of the other neighbours the next night. I breathed a sigh of relief and felt a huge surge of gratitude for the friendly people of the world.

My university degree was all but finished and I would soon have a qualification, albeit one that didn't open a lot of doors in terms of the workforce. I looked to the end of my studies with a great deal of sadness; I had loved the structure and challenge of being an art student and had no idea what I was going to do on leaving art school. My fantasy was to stay an extra year and complete my Honours, but there were 48 people in my class and only about ten places in the Honours course. Assessment came and I handed in all the work I had been working on recently – paintings, photos, videos and drawings. While most people had set up their studio as if it were a gallery, with one body of work for the lecturers to grade, I had put everything I'd done and was happy with all over my space; on the walls, on a table, on the floor. I could not think that one type of work was any better or worse than another, and, even if I could, I did not want to make the choice as to what was the more successful work just in case the lecturers hated it. After a short wait I got a letter from Monash offering me an interview for Honours. I was surprised when I checked my student e-mail account and saw my results – my lowest grade was 78 per cent and my highest 92 per cent. I had done better than ever before while at art school and had passed third year with an average score of over 80 per cent. A week after my interview I found out that I was to be an Honours student next year.

I could see the other people from my year accepted into Honours as deserving, but I could not apply the same rule to myself. In a way I still had some of my underconfidence from my time at RMIT when I was so sensitive and negative about my artistic ability that I actually cried at seeing a beautifully resolved artwork by a fellow student once. I still felt that I had no idea what I was actually doing art-wise and was surprised that anyone thought I was an exceptional student. I did read a lot of philosophy and had a better knowledge of art history than most, but my art was all writing and photography, messily done with simple ideas behind it.

Di was a woman in her forties in my class who I had told a lot of things about my life – even the fact I had Asperger Syndrome. She had won the prize for getting the top marks in the whole year for her final year and produced stunning artworks, mainly sculptural things using 'gross' materials such as jelly and rubber. I had become a bit fixated on Di and longed to speak to her every time I was at art school. I worried she would get a bit sick of me but, to my surprise, she always seemed happy to spend time with me. A few weeks into my degree I got used to the dynamics of the class and found I had people to talk to most of the time. I was amazed at how popular I seemed to have become. Only one person in the Honours class reacted to me badly, everyone else talked to me and invited me to openings of exhibitions they were putting on or asked me to go to the pub with them for beers. My address book, which had three people's addresses in for about a year after I was given it, was now full of phone numbers and addresses of people I could call and talk to whenever I liked. I had an exhibition at a university gallery and loads of people turned up to the opening – not just family members but friends. I couldn't believe that so many people liked to spend their time with me. I'd never been popular before.

I was also gaining respect for my abilities as an artist and had several shows lined up. I even got one show by just wandering into a gallery and showing the director some photos of the work I wanted to exhibit. She took a quick look and asked what month would suit me! Jenna, a woman about the same age as me who was also in the Honours class, asked myself, Di and another woman, Meriam, if we wanted to form an artist group to do experimental projects and performance art-type things. We started having regular meetings and inviting other artists to work with us. We were involved in a group exhibition at an experimental art space along with several successful artists. I was thrilled that my art career was going so well and started keeping a tally of how many shows I'd had during my Honours year, the number growing steadily as the months passed by. I was accepted for a video screening in the city centre on a huge outdoor screen, I organised a video exhibition at a screen gallery in the city, I participated in the first ever show at a new gallery. My artist's resumé was actually looking 'real' and was no longer comprised entirely of exhibitions put on at art school. I loved being an art student and happily looked forward to a future having exhibitions and going to openings with artist friends. I'd exorcised my demons and started to believe in myself as an artist.

At the beginning of my Honours year my grandma died at the age of 100. While it was a sad event, in a way it was a good thing. She had been very deaf and almost blind and all her friends had died, leaving her very lonely. When my dad and I had visited the previous year I had thought that her world had closed in and she had finally become old in her mind as well as her body. The woman who had accepted every-thing wisely, and had even written to her granddaughter in prison without judgement, had started to worry about petty things and criti-cise 'the young people', something she would never have done a few years earlier. As my biological grandparents were now all dead I started to think of my mum's stepmother, Pauline, as my grandmother and started calling her 'Grandma'. I had disliked Pauline when I was a socialist and thought the sophistication and good taste I had admired in her when we first met was a sign of bourgeois decadence. However, now that I was no longer filled with political fervour and judgement, I started to enjoy Pauline's company and her view of the world. I visited when I could and called my new grandma on the phone quite often. I was surprised to learn that Pauline would have loved me to call her Grandma from the first time we met.

My English grandma left some money for her children and grand-children in her will – an unexpected surprise. I received about $3000 and wondered what I could do to honour her memory with it. I decided to buy a new computer. I bought a new Macintosh computer and named it 'Esmerelda', an old lady's name to remind me of how I had been able to afford my beautiful new computer. I was now able to edit my videos at home and, the night after I brought Esmerelda home, I woke up at 4.30 am and edited a video just because I could. I saved up and bought a good video editing program and spent a week or so teaching myself how to use it. I got some work making videos for a Masters student at Monash and was amazed that she thought the productions I made for her were very professional and even more surprised when she offered me $50 an hour for the work I'd done. I hadn't had any paid work in ten years and had developed a bit of a phobia about being employed. The only time I'd worked in the last ten years was when I had a dishwashing job and had been so stressed about working that I'd ended up in psychiatric hospital. I now had the possibility of being self-employed to think about and I liked the idea a lot. If I screwed up it didn't matter anywhere near as much as if I did something wrong while working for a boss. I could always rework a video and not charge for the labour, anyway. Everyone told me what a good filmmaker I was.

I soon had another job possibility open up and it was one that challenged but excited me; I had a phone call while putting up some work in a gallery, a call from the manager of the autism employment service I had joined a couple of years before. He told me he wanted to set up a consultancy service whereby people with autism or Asperger Syndrome would present talks about their condition to government departments, health services and employers. He said he really wanted me for the position and that there would be training provided. I was nervous at the prospect of meeting a room full of people with Asperger Syndrome; I had only met two people in my life with the same diagnosis as me and had found one to be completely different from me and the other very irritating. As the university year ended I spent as much time worrying about the training for my possible position teaching others about Asperger Syndrome as I did my results for Honours.

I decided I wanted to go on to do Masters – I liked studying and it gave me the option of teaching at university level. I applied for Monash and for the course at RMIT. I spent weeks preparing my final piece for assessment, a huge installation pretty much telling the story of my life through written snippets of anecdotes and pictures, with a

TV showing a videotaped 'confession' to various things I'd done in my past ranging from the criminal to the petty. All the students thought my piece was fantastic and I was very happy with it. I thought I had a good chance of being accepted to do my Masters and for once was very confident. A few weeks after final assessment, results came out and I was horrified to see that I had been given a good but not fantastic mark, 72 per cent, for painting. This meant I was technically able to do Masters but unlikely to get in because of the competition for places. For the first time in my career at Monash I felt bitter and resentful toward my lecturers. I did not get a place in Monash's Masters programme. I went through the stages most people do when grieving a loved one and felt a bit guilty that I felt this way; it was only a university place, after all. After two days I had completely accepted the fact that I would probably not be studying during the next year and put my mind to finding some more filming work and thinking of new art projects to do. I was totally unprepared for the phone call from the head of Masters at the other institution, RMIT, to tell me I had an interview, and even less prepared for him telling me a few weeks later that I'd been accepted.

I was once again going to be a student at RMIT. I was not sure how I felt about returning to study there and kept taking the tram into the city centre to wander around the campus to get used to the idea. I was glad I would be in the postgraduate building as I was sure that returning to the other building where my studio had been in 1993 would bring back some memories I didn't want. I relived with nostalgia the feelings I'd had when walking past the markets from my house to RMIT and watched the people selling newspapers at the socialist bookstall, remembering my years doing exactly the same thing. I kept telling myself I was a different person now and that it could never be like it was all those years ago, but somehow I felt the same. After about two weeks of wandering around the university I seemed to come to terms with my memories and become the Jeanette of the present once more. I no longer felt that my life had a circular plot that would somehow take me back to where I had been. I was not the same me I had been then and had in fact gone through several versions of me in that time: socialist-Jeanette, criminal-Jeanette, drug addict-Jeanette, mentally ill-Jeanette and now, to myself. I was close to being just Jeanette and not needing to belong to a particular group with its own set of rules.

A neighbour, Gary, a man who prided himself on his honesty, told me he thought I was a liar because I changed from one version of me to another depending on who I was speaking to. I would be chatting with Gary in my best just-out-of-jail tones, complete with prison slang and swear words, and then the phone would ring and I would effortlessly switch to my art student voice. Without knowing how, I had become a chameleon who could change instantly to reflect my surroundings. I only seemed to be myself when in my own company, even though I now had my own views on life and my own rules; whenever someone else was around I always played a part.

I knew who I was but nobody else knew me properly. There was one person in my life who came close to knowing me and that was Rana. When I first met Rana I felt she was someone who already knew me. I was terrified. She knew all my secrets without me even saying them. I argued with everything she said to me, even if I actually agreed with her. I was sure I could throw her off the scent by being mean and disagreeing with every point she made. Patiently, she ignored my anger and arguments and kept coming to see me. After a couple of months I accepted her, giving up on my battle to keep her out. She visited every day and I soon knew her like I knew few other people. I would play with my fun things, pretty rocks, pieces of paper, pens, in front of her, not embarrassed that I was doing 'silly' things, 'immature' things that adults don't do. Rana put up with my literal interpretation of everything she said, letting me know she was 'only joking' every time I took offence to something she said that was meant in fun. While other friends had laughed *at* me for my perceived oddities, Rana laughed *with* me. I told her about my having Asperger Syndrome and, far from judging me or putting me down, she asked questions about my perception of the world and tried to involve me in her world. I shared my concerns about the fact that I was to meet a group of others with Asperger Syndrome and my worry that I would not be able to face seeing things about myself that I did not accept in others.

The first day I spent at the course run by the autism employment service, I was filled with emotion and wonder. There were 25 people in the room and it was like looking into a mirror; I saw elements of myself wherever I looked – a strange, fascinating, moving and wonderful thing. I met a woman called Donna who I took an instant like to. Everyone seemed to know her and I wanted to as well. I started chatting with her and asked what she did. She told me she was an author and that she ran workshops on autism, painted, sculpted and made music. I was a little in awe of Donna but thought her fun and generous and friendly. When I told her I made videos she told me she wanted to make some films and offered me a job. I asked Donna where I could buy a copy of one of her books and she told me she had stacks of copies at home.

I wanted to spend all my time with people with autism, people who thought similarly to me, who knew some of what I knew. Everyone in the course was different and individual, but all I could see was what we shared and the points at which we connected. I was no longer going to hide the fact that I had an autism spectrum condition, to be ashamed of it like it was some dirty, guilty thing I'd done that I didn't want people to know about. Asperger Syndrome was part of me – something I couldn't just ignore or discard, something I did not need to hide. My embarrassment was ridiculous, like being ashamed of the colour of your eyes or the length of your nose. Asperger Syndrome had shaped my personality as much as the family I was born into had, or the choices I had made in life. Denying it was like denying myself. I went home from the course unable to sleep. I invited Rana to come and chat to me. I needed to tell someone about the exciting and empowering day I'd had and thought that she would be the perfect person to tell.

I excitedly rang Rana and she rushed down from her flat just upstairs from mine to hear my news. I talked and talked for hours, telling of my happiness at meeting people like myself. I told her about my years of acting, my years of being who people wanted rather than

being myself, my years of surviving but not really living and of inhabiting so many worlds at once that I lost my ability to inhabit my own
inner world. I talked about my fear of people knowing me, my embarrassment at my own strangeness, my lack of friends for so long. I told
my friend about my years of living in prisons, both physical and
mental, and of hating myself for being different. I told Rana about my
art and how I'd never really felt I was any good at my chosen profes-
sion. I told her about my anxieties, my phobias and my insecurities,
how I'd been unable to work for so long. I talked about how I felt
wrong as the successful person I had become, that I was constantly surprised at all the good things in my life and at the fact that everything I
wanted seemed to happen. I talked until the early hours of the
morning, until it seemed that there was no more that needed saying. I
started playing, picking up a bottle of vitamins and dropping it on the
table, giggling and doing it over and over gleefully, marvelling at the
way it landed exactly the same way every time. I played and played,
Rana joining in the laughter.

A few weeks after meeting so many others with Asperger
Syndrome and autism, I started working for the author I had met,
Donna Williams, making films. With some of the money I'd made from
the films, I bought a copy of her first book, *Nobody Nowhere*, and read it
in a matter of days. I had never read anything like it and casually
blurted to Donna that maybe I should write my life story, too. To my
shock, she agreed with me instantly. As far as she was concerned it was
going to be a great book and well worth reading. After much deliberation and Donna's seemingly boundless optimism, I actually ended up
convinced I could do it and decided to start an autobiography.

I wrote the first chapter in a couple of days, but the moaning pessi-
mist in me still nagged that it would probably turn out to be another
project I started but never finished. The first few chapters were hard-
going but as soon as I reached the more difficult times in my past I felt
trapped with having to set all this free. There was only one thing to do:
I knew I needed to finish the thing. Donna's confidence in me was
unstoppable and she often discussed what I would do 'when it gets
published'. For two months my visual art took a back seat and I spent

every spare minute writing. In my mind I had a dream that the book would be published but in reality this prospect terrified me. I had put on paper things that even those closest to me didn't know and the act of writing had made them seem even more real, 'out there' and unretractable. Still, the moment I finished the last line I let out a triumphant yell and called Donna, excitedy telling her it was 'done'. Donna looked at the finished manuscript and within a week I had an edited version ready to send to a publisher. I was torn between wanting the world to read what I had written and wanting to hide the book away and only show it to those who were closest to me, but I sent the manuscript to the publisher.

The act of writing the book had forced me to accept a lot of things about myself that I had been in denial about and to take responsibility for all the choices I had made in the past, both good and bad. I knew I would never be quite the same as I was before writing the book and it almost felt like I'd lost any remaining innocence I may have had, any remaining capacity to fob off the severity of what I had done in the past, its impact on myself or others or that, however narrow the choices, the responsibility for my actions had always been mine.

I received the e-mail from the publisher. She was interested in my book. To have a book published was something anyone would see as being a sign of success, yet I did not feel successful. My view of myself was that of a prisoner or a drug addict; as someone who could not cope with life and who would never amount to anything. I would now have to re-assess how I saw myself.

The publisher wrote and talked about the content of my book. I felt naked, exposed and frightened. I'd given strangers an invitation to my private world. It was as if I was walking around the house in the nude with the curtains open and the lights on. I e-mailed Donna and told her how I felt, feeling grateful that she knew what I was going through. I knew I was going to have to learn to live with anonymous strangers knowing things about me that I had always kept hidden, but as far as I was concerned it was a small price to pay for the freedom to look at myself with acceptance and self-honesty.

Epilogue

The actor I once was is now past. I am almost able to be myself in most situations and many of the people who know me now know as close to a version of my true self as there is. I can finally say I actually quite like myself. It seems strange to be in a position where things seem to work out most of the time. I have to consciously remind myself that I am no longer the criminal, the drug addict or the disturbed person I was in the past. It seems that almost everything I have wanted to happen in the past couple of years has happened and yet this leaves me feeling just a little guilty, as if maybe I deserve some hard times. Like negative situations, positive things also have to be dealt with and understood.

I tend to think that we are all given a set of circumstances to deal with and that we have to do the best with what we have at our disposal. I was given a bit of a dud hand in life, but I've done what I can with it. I have no idea about things like reading facial expressions and do not know what eyes are saying. I rarely understand other people's motivations and have to work such things out through their actions. I have many anxieties about life and seem to think I have to be the best at what I do to be appreciated. I am, however, quite happy. I fit into the world to which I was born. I am comfortable to be a woman with Asperger Syndrome who has had a somewhat dark and bizarre life. I see my understanding of logic and reason and my dedication to whatever I put my mind to as an enormous advantage. If I had the choice to see the world the way most people see it and to have the understanding and communication skills of the majority, I would not take it. I look forward to what lies ahead with great interest and enthusiasm.